Advice to a Desolate France

Sebastian Castellio

Introduction and Notes by Marius F. Valkhoff

Translated by Wouter Valkhoff

Preface by Albert Geyser

ACTONINSTITUTE

Advice to a Desolate France

© 2016 by Acton Institute

Originally published 1562 as *Conseil à la France désolée*. New edition with preface and explanatory notes published 1967. English translation published 1975 by Patmos Press. Reprinted with permission.

Cover image: Moord op de protestanten te Wassy, 1562 and Serie 3: Franse Godsdienstoorlogen, 1559–1573, by Frans Hogenberg
Source: Europeana via Rijksmuseum, public domain: http://www.europeana.eu/portal/en/record/90402/RP_P_OB_78_784_24.html

Author image: Sebastian Castellio
Source: Wikimedia Commons, https://commons.wikimedia.org/wiki/File:Sebastian_Castellio_-_anonym.jpg

ISBN: 978-1-942503-41-5

ACTONINSTITUTE

98 E. Fulton
Grand Rapids, Michigan 49503
Phone: 616.454.3080
Fax: 616.454.9454
www.acton.org

Interior design by Judy Schafer
Cover design by Peter Ho

Printed in the United States of America

Contents

Preface

Such was the legacy of intolerance and intransigence left by the Religious Wars that for the succeeding almost four hundred years, neither Catholic nor Protestant scholars had the time or the ear for the few voices of moderation from those distant stormy times.

Moreover, those prophetic messages of moderation and tolerance could only become audible in our ecumenical atmosphere, and this last only became apparent, amongst Protestants and Catholics alike, since the last World War.

At the time and in the heat of the struggle, both Catholics and Calvinists rejected advocates of tolerance as harmful to their respective holy causes. They persecuted them as liberalists and burnt their books as heretical. They did this last with such application that very few copies of these pleas were left.

It is to the honour of Buisson, Giran, Lecler, Bainton, Becker, Delormeau, and now Valkhoff that by diligent research they retrieved these works and revived the memory of their heroic authors. Valkhoff's fully documented and annotated edition of Castellio's *Advice to a Desolate France,* not only contributes materially to the historical knowledge of that forgotten but meaningful side of the Religious Wars, but also makes it easily accessible to the English reader.

Rejected by their contemporaries and buried by subsequent generations, men like Castellio have meaningful advice even for our twentieth century. His work and that of Pasquier need to be republished exactly now, for reasons as valid now as in their times. Doctrinal intolerance, in their day, had claimed hundred thousands of lives; ideological intolerance, its blood brother in more senses than one, in our day claimed the lives of millions, and is still savaging many in most countries.

Ideological intolerance, whether racial, national or social, reveals all the symptoms of religious doctrinalism. It demands absolute conformity, it forces and violates the consciences of dissidents, slanders them, brands them as heretics and traitors and liberalists, hounds them and kills them.

Castellio's arguments against this lethal mass madness are as valid today as four centuries ago. He based them on Scripture, common sense, common law, and natural law. He addresses them to priests, pastors, politicians, princes and the common people. He reminds them of the demonstrable truth that "tyranny engenders sedition," that a forced and violated conscience turns to hatred, and that the "remedial" suppression of freedom of speech and thought kills, but never cures. He reminds them of the example of prophets and Apostles who persuaded by truth, but never forced, and of Christ who came not to destroy, but to save, and who taught the immutably true: Do unto others, what you want them to do unto you.

Valkhoff's clarifying notes both to the text and the historical circumstances which produced it, enhance the value of this little jewel of sublime argument for the scholar as well as for the man in search of direction in our world of propaganda and ideological intolerance.

—Albert Geyser

Introduction to the French Edition

At the end of the year 1562, when France was in the midst of a religious war, a small book of 96 pages in 12° was published anonymously, without any indication of the place where it was published. Its title was *Advice to a Desolate France,* but its sub-title gives an eloquent summary of the contents. As early as 1563 some copies had reached the Calvinist Republic of Geneva, where the farrier, Michel Chatillon, interrogated by the Consistory, confessed that they had been sent to him from Basle, by his cousin, the printer Ph. Chapuis. The matter concerned a copy for himself and another meant for his uncle, Mathieu Eyssautier, a heterodox priest, who had been banished from the city. The treatise had been written by Michel's uncle, Sebastian Castellio, professor of Greek at the university of Basle, the very man who is considered by our contemporaries as the great precursor of liberal Protestantism. The members of the Church Council judged it "full of error," reprimanded the importers, and ordered the destruction of the available copies.[1]

It is therefore not surprising that only very few copies of this little masterpiece have survived until our time; we only

---

[1]   See Ferdinand Buisson, *Sébastien Castellion. Sa vie et son oeuvre* (1515–1563), *Etudes sur les origines du Protestantisme libéral français*, Paris, 1892, vol. 11, pp. 225ff.

know of four.[2] Although Castellio's two biographers, Ferdinand Buisson[3] and Etienne Giran[4] have published large extracts of the *Advice*, the preparation of a complete edition, more than four centuries after its first publication, is by no means a superfluous endeavour. In this edition we have, as far as possible, preserved the language and spelling of the period, not wishing to modernise the original text. Only, as we wished this work to be read, we have corrected printer's errors, added accents, normalised the punctuation and explained certain archaic words and expressions in footnotes. Our edition, therefore, presents Castellio's own text, rendered, we hope, somewhat more accessible to the non-specialised reader.

The beginning of the 1560s was decisive for the political and religious history of a France torn by the struggles between Protestants and Catholics. After the death of Henri II (in 1559), we witness a change of opinion: instead of persecuting the "heretics," the government first inclines towards a policy of conciliation and later on manifests a certain measure of tolerance. As early as the reign of Catherine de Medici, influenced by her chancellor, Michel de L'Hospital, we witness the beginnings of these new tendencies.

Castellio himself, in his book, mentions three important events, which took place shortly before its publication: the Conspiracy of Amboise, the January Edict and the Massacre of Wassy. These are well-known historical events, and we shall therefore describe them but briefly. What interests us in this

---

[2] Namely at the Library of the British Museum, at the National Library and the Library of the Society of the History of French Protestantism, in Paris, and in the Public and University Library at Geneva.

[3] Buisson, *op. cit.*

[4] Etienne Giran, *Sébastien Castellion et la Réforme Calviniste: Les deux Réformes*, Haarlem, Paris, 1914.

instance is the atmosphere in which they took place and also the *Advice*, which they inspired to a large extent.

In the Conspiracy of Amboise, one must see a reaction against the religious persecutions of the reign of Henri II. Certain Protestant gentlemen and their co-religionists tried to bring the new king, the young François II, under their influence, in order to impose their ideas on him and to prevent the return of the cruelties of the preceding reign (under the influence of the Guises). The undertaking failed lamentably and the many conspirators were virtually all massacred. At the end of his long life, the poet Agrippa d'Aubigné would still remember how, when a young boy, his father showed him the flower of Protestant youth betrayed and hung ignobly from the balconies of the castle of Amboise by the Catholic government.

The January Edict (1562), in authorising Protestant religious services outside the cities, and condoning family worship, was like a balm on the recent wounds. But it neither satisfied the fanatics of the one, nor of the other movement. For the Catholics the concessions were too far-reaching, whereas the Protestants found them ineffective and insufficient. Nevertheless, in the climate of the time, the January Edict represented a first manifestation of tolerance, and as such constituted a great step forward.

Meanwhile both parties were consolidating their respective positions, whilst arming themselves to the teeth. It was therefore but a question of time before a spark would set off the explosion. This indeed happened very soon: on the 1st of March, 1562, the duke François de Guise, accompanied by an armed escort, passed through the small town of Wassy in Champagne. They discovered a Protestant assembly listening to their preacher's sermon in a barn. The soldiers of the duke started to insult the Protestants, and finally opened fire. A general battle ensued, and in this way some sixty men and women were killed and a further hundred injured.

Even at that time, the matter could have been peacefully settled and Théodore de Bèze, Calvin's right hand man at Geneva, in fact suggested this. But Condé and the other leaders, Protestant as well as Catholic, pressed for war. Soon they were swept along by their own supporters, and hostilities broke out spontaneously in various parts of France. Like all civil wars, this one too was accompanied by horrible atrocities, which were committed by both sides. To gain some idea of these happenings, it suffices to read the memoirs of the period or to evoke such personalities as the Catholic Monluc or the Protestant des Adrets.

Psychologically, one can explain the fury of this war. For many years, the Protestants had allowed themselves be led to the stake to be burnt there, like victims of some ancient sacrifice, guilty at most of what we might today call an offense against conventional beliefs. In one of his works, Castellio depicts the following moving scene: the wife and children of a condemned man in the middle of the crowd on the public square, witnessing in despair and with eyes bathed in tears, the agony of their husband and father. One understands that after so many similar scenes the Protestants had reached the end of their tether. The Catholics, on their part, became more and more alarmed at the ever increasing acts of vandalism, committed by Protestant iconoclasts. Outside the churches, the harquebusiers shot at the sculptures and stained-glass windows; inside pillagers broke the crucifixes, threw down and demolished the statues of the Holy Virgin and the saints, and desecrated the altars and hosts. "The pomp of the catholic ceremonies, the decoration of the altars, the blood-covered Christs crowned with thorns, the saints represented in their tribulations and triumphs, all these spectacles, all these enchantments of the imagination and the eyes, appeared as idolatries, remnants of paganism, to the followers of Calvin."[5]

It goes without saying that in the course of the wars of religion, the Catholics were not the only ones to exterminate defenceless adversaries. Priests, monks, nuns and ordinary faithful were certainly not spared. Corresponding to the massacre of Wassy in the North, we have the "Michelade" in the South, during which, on the morning after St. Michael's of the year 1567, a band of Protestants executed eighty laymen, priests and worshippers in the courtyard of the Bishop's Palace at Nimes.[6]

In this atmosphere of unchained emotions, one man only managed to retain his calm and to plead eloquently for an appeasement of the passions—Castellio. The *Advice* is a pacifist and at the same time an ecumenical manifesto. The author attempts to remain completely objective—a rare occurrence in that period. Also, in conformity with the edicts of pacification, he avoids the injurious epithets "papists" and "huguenots." In the twentieth century the author Romain Rolland was to display the same courage, and during the First World War braved public opinion in the warring countries with his manifesto *Au-dessus de la mêlée*.[7] He was obliged to take refuge in Switzerland, but was compensated for his independence of spirit by the award of the Nobel prize. Similarly Castellio was violently attacked by the opposing parties of his time, and he was totally unable to influence the course of events. The present work did, however, earn him the esteem of posterity.

---

[5] Ernest Lavisse, *Histoire de France depuis les origines jusqu'à la Révolution.* Vol. VI. 1. La Réforme et la Ligue. L'Edit de Nantes (1559–1598) by Jean H. Mariéjol, Paris, 1904, p. 64.

[6] Joseph Lecler, *Histoire de la Tolérance au siècle de la Réforme,* Vol. 11, Paris, 1955, p. 2.

[7] "Above the battle-field."

The fundamental work on Castellio remains that of F. Buisson (see footnote 1), which is supplemented by the works of Roland H. Bainton and Bruno Becker. Above all, we are thinking of the translation and commentary of the *Traité des hérétiques* by the first mentioned, and the discovery of two manuscripts of Castellio by the second.[8] But we also wish to bring to the reader's attention the recent biography *Sébastien Castellion Apôtre de la Tolerance et de la Liberté de Conscience* by Charles E. Delormeau.[9] Even if this author does not really reveal anything new, he does nevertheless present a good synthesis.

The six French works of Castellio constitute but a minor part of his total output, the complete bibliography of which is given by Buisson towards the end of the second volume of his monograph (see footnote 1). But if Castellio survives as one of the classical authors who is read—and will still be read—in the course of this century, this is largely due to his activities as a French writer. His first book, a scholastic Latino-French manual, the *Dialogues sacrés* (1543),[10] was a best seller in Germany during the 17th and 18th centuries. Its success was due to the fact that Castellio had created a Latin literature at the level of young pupils, based on stories of the Bible, rather than the pagan Latin authors who were often either too difficult or too frivolous for them. The following volumes of this manual were written exclusively in Latin. Between his first book and his last, namely our *Advice to a Desolate France,* we find four other works: the *Traité des hérétiques* (1554), about which further mention will be made further on, the *Bible en français* (1555), written in the popular French of

---

[8] Roland H. Bainton, *Concerning Heretics,* New York, 1935. Bruno Becker, *Un manuscrit inédit de Castellion, in Castellioniana,* Leyde, 1951, pp. 101–111.

[9] Neuchâtel (1965).

[10] A photographic re-edition of the 1st volume of the *Dialogues sacrés* is in existence at the Fischbacher Library in Paris, 1932.

the period, an extremely original work, of which several frag-
ments deserve to be included in a future anthology of Castellio,
his translation of the *Theologia Deutsch* (1558), preceded by an
important preface of the translator,[11] and the French text of his
last defense of liberty of conscience and free investigation (*De
haereticis a civili magistratu non puniendis...*) which, though not
written by his own hand, he may have partially dictated and of
which he revised at least a third.[12]

The three principal works, the *Traité des hérétiques, De l'impunité
des hérétiques*—this is how we have baptized the French version of the treatise mentioned in the preceding paragraph—
and even the *Advice to a Desolate France,* were all inspired by a
contemporary event, namely the execution of Michel Servet, on
the 27th October, 1553. When this Spanish doctor and anti-
trinitarian theologian had been burnt alive at Champel near
Geneva, after a theological trial conducted by Jean Calvin, the
Protestant world was appalled at this act of intolerance. This
time it was no longer a matter of a Protestant condemned by
the Catholic Inquisition, or a revolutionary Anabapist put to
death by the tribunal of some German prince, but now it was a
victim of the Reformation, an honest man, whose only wrong
was to have differed in opinion with the Reformed orthodox
Church. Critics were numerous, and Calvin was obliged to
defend his position. The only man who, thereupon, had the
courage to contradict and even accuse the powerful reformer in
writing, was Castellio.

---

[11] We have re-edited Castellio's Preface as the Introduction to an
anthology of chapters in the translation by Pierre Poiret: *La Théologie
Germanique* (Haarlem 1950).

[12] These are the two unknown manuscripts discovered by Becker (see
further on). With his approval, we have prepared a philological
edition of the French version.

We can thus distinguish three stages in the famous controversy which followed:

1. Barely four months after the execution of Servet, Calvin published both in Latin and in French his *Déclaration pour maintenir la vraie foi*.[13] Some days later appeared, both in Latin and in French, the *Traité des hérétiques* by Castellio, under the name of Martin Bellie, with a fictitious editor. It was therefore not a direct answer to Calvin's treatise, but an independent attack against the reformer's intolerance, in the form of an anthology of passages selected from the works of defenders of liberty of conscience, amongst others Luther and Calvin themselves, writing in their earlier years.

2. Castellio now had a text which he could refute argument by argument, and he did not hesitate to do just this. Because of Calvin's interventions with the Council of Basle, however, the *Contra libellum Calvini*[14] could not appear during Castellio's lifetime. It was only in 1612 that the Netherlands Remonstrants (or Arminians), who were waging an identical battle against the intransigence of the official Calvinists (or Gomarists), published the treatise and in so doing saved it from oblivion. At the same time that Castellio replied to Calvin, Théodore de Bèze, Calvin's faithful collaborator and, later, his successor at Geneva, had published a Latin refutation of the *Traité des hérétiques* (entitled *De haereticis a civili magistratu puniendis libellus, adversus Martini Belli farraginem et novorum Academicorum sectam*[15]), which was thereafter translated into French by Nicolas Colladon. Because of Castellio's pseudonym this book is generally known as the *Anti-Bellius*. The repercussions of this polemic were such

---

[13] "Declaration to maintain the true Faith."

[14] "Against Calvin's book."

[15] "Book proving that heretics should be punished by the magistrate, against Martin Bellius' nonsense talk against the sect of the new Academics."

that for a long time the liberal movement and the defenders of tolerance were respectively known as *Bellianism* and *Bellianists*.

3. Castellio thus seemed to have been effectively refuted by the astute arguments of Bèze, to which the Council of Basle forbade him to reply. But truth and justice always triumph in the end. In 1938, Bruno Becker, the well-known Dutch specialist on the 16th century, discovered what we could perhaps now call Castellio's swan song, in the small library of the Remonstrant community in Rotterdam. It consisted of two manuscripts, one in Latin and the other in French. The title of the first repeated that of Bèze's treatise virtually word for word, adding only a *non:*[16] *De haereticis a civili magistrate non puniendis, pro Martini Bellii farragine, adversus Theodori Bezae libellus, Authore Basilio Montfortio,* and is in fact a thorough refutation of it (see note 8, the cited article by Becker). Thus, when these manuscripts will be published after four centuries—which will be done, we hope, in the relatively near future—the 20th century reader will be able to transport himself to the 1550s, and to evoke anew the famous controversy.

In the meantime, the *Advice to a Desolate France,* which contains several reminiscences of this great religious and philosophical quarrel, may serve as an introduction to the subject.

Sebastian Castellio was a revolutionary of the spiritual life, very much like Dirk Goornhert in Holland, a quarter of a century later. Both abound in modern ideas, are far ahead of their time, and are still very much up to date even now. In each of his French works, to quote but these, Castellio introduces something new.[17] In the manifesto which we are publishing, his defense of the individual conscience and the respect which one owes to its mystery and liberty, have led Father Joseph

---

[16] "Not."

[17] See our *Chronique Castellionienne*, in *Neophilologus*, XLII, 1958, pp. 277–288.

Lecler to describe him as a *personalist,* even before the term had been coined.[18] For the rest, it is in this personalism that the *Advice* rather differs from its model, which Castellio does not fail to mention, namely the *Exhortation aux Princes* of 1561.[19]

As early as 1892, the historian Alfred Rambaud wrote these enthusiastic lines: "Why should the works of Castellio, at least his French works, not find an editor? Why not, between these two intolerant men of genius, Calvin and Bossuet, make a place for a writer who is far closer to us in his outlook, to the author of the preface to the 'Traité des hérétiques' and of the 'Advice to a Desolate France'? It would be right for Castellio to come to the fore and plead his own cause, no longer before the Basle Senate, but before this new France, before this new humanity, the advent of which he has helped to prepare."[20]

In 1913, the *Traité des hérétiques,* to which Castellio, by the way, contributed far more than the mere preface, was re-edited by A. Olivet and prefaced by J. Eugène Choisy (Geneva, A. Jullien). Unfortunately, this editor not only modernised the orthography, but also the language and, what is worse, has committed a great number of errors in the transcription.[21]

---

[18] Lecler, *op. cit.* 11, p. 67.

[19] Etienne Pasquier, *Exhortation aux Princes et Seigneurs du Conseil privé du Roy, pour obvier aux séditions qui semblent nous menacer pour le fait de la Religion.* J. Lecler has contested the traditional attribution of this work to Etienne Pasquier (*op. cit.*, 11, pp. 43, 44), but Dorothy Thickett, in turn, has refuted this; see her *Bibliographie des oeuvres d'Etienne Pasquier* Geneva, 1956, pp. 77–78.

[20] Giran, *op. cit.,* p. v.

[21] See our article *Sebastien Castellion et l'idee de la tolerance,* in *Castellioniana,* Leyde, 1951, p. 82, 1.

Thanks to the present edition, the reader will be able to enjoy this other little masterpiece by Castellio, the *Advice to a Desolate France*. May this text contribute to give its author the place which he deserves in the history of ideas![22]

—Marius F. Valkhoff
University of the Witwatersrand, Johannesburg

[22] At the end of this Introduction, we would like to thank most sincerely Mr. Alain Dufour for having read and perfected our manuscript, and Professor Albert Geyser for having helped us to find or to verify Castellio's biblical quotations.

Advice to a Desolate France

Sebastian Castellio

The Malady of France

May a phial of the wrath of God now be poured and spread over your head, O desolate France. This wrath is so evident and touches you so closely, that it is no longer necessary to hold a long discourse to make you believe in it. For, considering that God is accustomed to punish with war, plague or famine, or two of these, or all three together, those who evoke His anger, you can see and feel that He castigates you with at least one of these, namely war (not to mention the other two, which are not far from your shoulders either). A war, indeed, so horrible and detestable that I do not know whether there ever was a worse one since the earth came into existence, even though the world has hardly ever been without war. For they are not strangers, those who are fighting you, as was the case in the past when, being attacked from the outside, you at least found some solace at home in the love and unity of your children. But this time your own children are ravaging and afflicting you, not by bickering with each other within your womb, as was the case with Rebecca, but by murdering and strangling each other within your bosom, without any mercy whatsoever, with enormous swords, fully drawn, with pistols and with halberds.

Well do you understand, O France, what I am saying, you who were so flourishing in the olden days, but are so strife-torn now. Well do you feel the blows and wounds which you are receiving, whilst your children are so cruelly killing one another. Well do you see that your towns and villages, indeed, your paths and fields, are littered with corpses, which stain your rivers red and putrify and foul the air. Briefly, within you there is neither peace nor rest, day nor night, and are but wails and lamentations heard from all sides and cannot a safe place, free of terror and murder, fear and horror, be found. This is your ill, O France, this is the malady which leaves you no respite, which torments you day and night.

The Seeking of a Remedy

Now we must see whether, somewhere in the world, the advice and remedy to heal you can be found. Many a time have I thought about this myself, and I was long in doubt as to whether I should apply myself to this, considering the difficulty which presented itself to me, not so much in the giving of good and definite advice (for that, unless I am very much deluding myself, is, thank God, rather easy for me), but in making it acceptable to those without whose consent I cannot see it being put into effect. And I would indeed, for the moment, have abstained from this undertaking, were it not for the magnitude of your ill, an ill so great, and becoming so much worse from day to day, that it is better for me to risk any possible consequences and at least do my duty, than to let you perish in such a miserable manner. For who knows whether the Lord might not wish to succour in just this way? Or, if this work is not of general benefit, it may be of advantage to someone in particular. When a house is burning, everyone hastens to it, so that, if it cannot be saved in its entirety, some or other item can at least be rescued from it, which is better than nothing. It may happen in like manner with this work, in that, if everyone does not turn over a new leaf, at least someone will, and in that way then, my work will not at all have been in vain.

Whatever the case may be, I am going to try to give you advice. May God grant that it will be to His Praise, and to your benefit, for I know well that unless He takes a hand in it, it will be a lost effort for me and for all mankind. Now, in order to find a remedy for you, it is necessary to do the same as good doctors do, who, in order to heal an illness, always seek the cause and then apply contrary remedies, in accordance with the general rule, which is that illnesses are healed by their antidotes. Likewise it is necessary, in this matter, to seek out the cause of your malady and then to apply contrary remedies to it. Otherwise, whatever one may do about it, will but be like beautiful plasters which, even whilst covering the wound on the outside, will nourish rather than heal it on the inside.

The Cause of the Malady

I find that the principal and effective cause of your malady, that is to say of the sedition and war which torment you, is the forcing of consciences, and I think that if you consider this well, you will assuredly find that this is so. As one had for a long time forced and tried to force the consciences of the Evangelics,[1] these first of all organized the Amboise Venture,[2] in the course of which their aims and intentions were discovered. As the result of this, they thoroughly provoked their opponents and rendered themselves very much suspect in their eyes. Since then various events have taken place, in particular the January Edict,[3] by which the States General attested that the Evangelics could

---

[1] Protestants.

[2] See Introduction, p. vi.

[3] *Ibid.*, pp. vi–vii.

hold their sermons outside the towns, and that none should hinder them. But this Edict pleased neither party, and least of all the Catholics, who acted in such a manner at the Massacre of Wassy and other massacres that this sedition or deadly war, call it what you may, resulted from it. I understand, indeed, that some Evangelics are going around saying that they did not take up arms for the sake of religion, but in order to maintain the said Edict. But let them give as many excuses as they like, since the Edict itself was proclaimed as the result of religion, and since the massacre at Wassy (as the result of which the Evangelics revolted) took place because of religion, and since, thereafter, churches were taken and pillaged and statues destroyed, it is better to confess to the truth without any pretences and to admit that, however many other things may be involved, the principal cause of this war is nevertheless the desire to preserve religion. And, if the January Edict had, in fact, been proclaimed on a subject matter not concerning religion, I indeed think that the Evangelics (and they themselves, I feel, would admit this to me) would not have been so quick and diligent to start such a large and dangerous revolt. I do not even want to mention that they themselves, in their treaty entered into at Orleans,[4] stress sufficiently clearly that they are fighting for religion, considering that of the three reasons for which they say they are taking up arms, the first is the Honour of God. As such, one must conclude that the cause of this war is the forcing of consciences.

Wrong Remedies

Now the remedy which your children, O France, are seeking is, firstly, to make war with each other, to kill and murder one another and, what is worse, to go and fetch money and men from foreign nations in order to resist still better, or rather in

---

[4]   In May 1562, at the start of the first war of religion.

order to avenge their brothers still better and, secondly, to force one another's consciences.

Those are the remedies which your children, O poor France, seek for your malady. They are, however, so unlike real remedies that they are having exactly the opposite effect, for these are the correct means to disembowel and destroy you, bodily as well as spiritually. For as far as the first is concerned, it is well known that foreigners who lend a helping hand to one or the other party in such sedition, are generally not quite so charitable that they do not, if not altogether, at least partly have regard for their own profit, as much or more so than for that of the other party. The result is that when the opportunity presents itself, they quite frequently say: "This piece will be good for us." And if that should happen to you today, O France (and the world is, as a matter of fact, not so very good that one might not have reason to suspect this), you would be the most torn and dismembered country that ever has been. For, as different kinds of help are coming to you from different quarters, I leave it to you to reason in what a state you would be if everyone should perchance come to take for himself.

It is not just as from today that such tricks are being played, and that help from foreigners in such disagreements has been more of a hindrance than of profit. One could quote many examples of this, but for the moment I shall content myself with two, of which one will be drawn from abroad and the other from your own country. The example from abroad concerns the ancient dispute about the reign of Judea, which took place there between two brothers, Hyrcan and Aristobulus, about 70 years before the birth of our Saviour, Jesus Christ. In this dispute Pompeius, Captain of the Romans, who was at that time in those parts, having been called in by them to assist them, helped them to such an extent that he subjugated Judea to the Romans and made it a tributary, which subjugation and serfdom have lasted until this day. The second example, taken from your own country, concerns those of Auvergne and Autun, who were, at the time of Julius Caesar, the most important tribes in the two belts of land in which the entire Gaul was divided, and who had a dispute amongst themselves as to who should be the rulers. The Auvergnats and the Bourguignons then proceeded to ask the Alamanni for help against those of Autun, which help the Alamanni gave them by subjugating and maltreating both the one party as well as the other, until such time as Julius Caesar, after having defeated Ariovistus, the King of the Alamanni, really delivered both of them from their subjection. This was done in such a manner, though, that they themselves and the other Gauls were finally both made subjects of the Romans. That, indeed, is often the result of foreign help in a dispute concerning the various peoples of a common country.

These examples are sufficiently adequate, O France, to cause you to fear a similar occurrence. And if I am answered that one also finds examples of the opposite happening, through which it can be shown that such foreign assistance has sometimes been beneficial, I answer that this is quite true. But the bad generally occurs more frequently than the good, and the world is so corrupt today, that one now has more occasion than ever to fear the bad. But let us assume that there is no danger at all in this regard, and that those whom one calls to aid are such good and loyal people that they have no regard whatsoever for their own profit and interest. I nevertheless say that so much blood will flow (for, without blood, such a war certainly cannot take place) that its loss will be irremediable. Indeed, what am I saying: It will flow? I say that so much of it has already flown (for it is said that more than fifty thousand persons have been put to death in France this summer) that I do not know whether as much good can ever come from this war (however happy its outcome may be) as the degree of evil which has already resulted from it. This so much so, that the human remedy which your children are seeking for your malady is no more suitable for curing it than if, in order to heal a sick body, one made every kind of thorough effort to cut off all its members.

Now as far as the spiritual remedy is concerned, which is the forcing of consciences, I cannot wonder enough (and I must speak frankly here) at the foolishness and blindness as much of the one side as of the other. And in order to make myself better understood, I want to address myself frankly to both parties for a while. Today there are two kinds of people in France who wage war amongst each other for the sake of religion. The first are called Papists by their adversaries and the others Huguenots, and the Huguenots call themselves Evangelics, and the Papists Catholics. I shall call them what they call themselves, in order not to offend them.

To the Catholics

First of all I want to talk to you, O Catholics, who claim to have the ancient, true and catholic faith and religion. Do consider your affairs somewhat closely for a while, for it is time and more than time that you should do so. Remember how you have hitherto treated the Evangelics. You know well that you have persecuted them, imprisoned them, locked them into subterranean cellars, let them be eaten by lice and fleas, let them rot in mud pits, kept them in hideous dark places, under the shadow of death, and finally roasted them alive on a small fire in order to prolong their sufferings even further. And for what crime? Because they did not want to believe in the Pope, or mass, or purgatory and such other things, all of which so completely lack any foundation in the Scriptures, that even their names are nowhere to be found in them. Is that not a beautiful and just reason for burning people alive? You call yourselves Catholics and make it your business to uphold the Catholic faith, as contained in the Holy Scriptures, but you nevertheless hold for heretics, and burn alive, those who only want to believe that which is contained in the Scriptures?

Stop a while here and weigh this up to the best of your knowledge. It is a point which is of great importance to you. Tell me and answer now, for you will, for better or for worse, in any event have to answer for it one day, before the just Judge, whose name you carry. Answer, I say, to a point which you will, without a doubt, be asked on the Day of Judgment. Would you yourselves like to be treated in this manner? Would you like to be persecuted, imprisoned, locked in subterranean cellars, given as food to lice and fleas, to rot in mud pits, to be kept in hideous dark places and under the shadow of death and, finally, to be roasted alive on a small fire, for not having believed in or confessed to something which was against your conscience? What do you answer? But what need is there for an answer; it is well known that your conscience says no, so emphatically indeed that even the most impudent amongst you would not dare to deny it.

Now consider this point well. If already in this life, full of ignorance and carnal influences, which very often cloud man's understanding, this truth nevertheless has such efficacy that it forces you, whether you want to or not, to confess that you have done to others something other than that which you would like to be done to you, what will it be like on the Day of Judgment, when all things will be clearly and vividly discovered and revealed? And do you not know that men's consciences will accuse or excuse each one at the Day of the just Judgment? And do you know whether the injustice which you have done to your brothers is small? It is, indeed, so small that they preferred to endure all the evils which your cruelty (I must, in truth, call it this) managed to invent, rather than (as you required) to do something which was against their consciences. And this is proof that to force a person's conscience is worse than to deprive him cruelly of his life, for a God-fearing person prefers to have himself cruelly deprived of his life rather than to let his conscience be forced.

Let us now discuss the practical experience, and here I shall take you yourselves as witnesses. There have been and are certain Evangelics who want to force you to go to their sermons, and I ask you how this violence pleases you? Without any doubt it displeases you, and you say that you are being done a great injustice, and still your conscience cannot be so hurt by hearing a sermon as that of an Evangelic is by hearing mass. Learn from your own consciences not to force those of others, and if you cannot support a small wrong, do not do a greater one to another. And know that the suffering which is now oppressing you, is the just wrath and judgment of God on you, Who is rendering you the like, and measuring you with the same measure with which you have measured, in accordance with what is written in the Scriptures: "He that leadeth into captivity shall go into captivity: he that killeth with the sword must be killed with the sword."[5] Likewise also: "Thou art righteous, O Lord, which art, and wast, and shalt be, because thou hast judged thus. For they have shed the blood of saints and prophets, and thou hast given them blood to drink; for they are worthy."[6] Because you have certainly martyred and murdered many a holy person, for which the Lord has now begun to reward you, and if you do not make amends, do not expect Him to withdraw His hand, which is stretched out to strike you. But how are you making amends? By doing even worse things than previously, namely by persecuting the Evangelics even more than ever. Is this the way to appease God? Is this not quite to the contrary, the very way to anger Him even more? For if He is angry with you by reason of your past cruelties (as, indeed, He is, and you are really blind if you do not see this), do not expect to appease Him by

5 Apoc. 13:10.

6 Apoc. 16:5–6.

persevering with the same cruelty. For you are acting just like the man who has contracted gout by drinking too much, and then proceeds to drink even more, in order to get rid of it. Or like a child which has been hit by its father for having hit its brother and which then, in order to appease its father, proceeds to hit its brother even harder.

To the Evangelics

Now I am coming to you, Evangelics. In the past you peaceably suffered persecution for the sake of the Gospel, loved your enemies and rendered good for evil. You blessed those who cursed you, resisting them in no other way than by fleeing, if necessary, and all this you did in accordance with the commandment of the Lord. From where, now, comes such a great change in some of you? The innocent will not feel offended at my words; I am not speaking to all. I am only addressing those who are as I have described, and to them I say: Has the Lord changed His commandment, and have you received a new revelation telling you to do exactly the opposite of what you did before? You began well in spirit, but how did you manage to succeed in the flesh?

He who formerly commanded you to endure, and to render right for wrong, and whom you then obeyed in enduring, and in rendering right for wrong, has He now commanded you to render wrong for wrong, and to persecute others, instead of enduring persecution? Or have you now turned your back on His commandment, and do you henceforth want to shake His yoke off your shoulders and live as it pleases you, by following the world, your minds and your enemies? For what else can one think, when you exchange all your possessions and even those of the poor, for halberds and harquebuses, when you kill and massacre your enemies and put them to the point of the sword, when you fill and besmirch the paths and streets, and even the houses and temples, with the blood of those for whom, like for yourselves, Christ has died, and who, like you, have been baptized in His name?

What more can I say but that you are forcing them against their consciences to attend your sermons and, what is worse, that you are forcing some to take up arms against their own brothers and those of their own religion.

Furthermore you question people on your doctrine and you are not satisfied with the fact that there is agreement on the main points of religion which are clear and evident from the Holy Scriptures. You then, if they are in agreement with you on all points, give them letters with which they can prove that they are faithful, that is to say Christians, wherever they may go, so that they may be recognized amongst the unfaithful. Those are the three remedies which you are using, namely bloodshed, the forcing of consciences, and the condemning and regarding as unfaithful of those who are not entirely in agreement with your doctrine, I am astounded at your lack of understanding if you do not see that you are following your enemies and him you usually call the Antichrist, in these three points.

I well understand that which some of you have taken to replying: namely that you are right, and they are wrong, and that for that reason it is quite permissible to persecute and force them. But they are not permitted to do this to you, which is the same as if you said that it is quite permissible for you to seize the possessions of others, but that others may not seize yours. But embellish your cause as much as you wish before men, and seek as many beautiful distinctions as you like, it is well known, and I am taking your own consciences as witnesses for this, that you are doing things to others which you would not like to be done to you. For if you were Papists, as you call them, and which most of you once were, you would certainly not like to be done to you what you are doing to them. And if today, whilst still in doubt as to who will be the victor, indeed whilst still being persecuted, you are nevertheless displaying such severity and violence, it is to be feared that if you should attain to your expectations, you would resort to just such great tyranny as your enemies have used.

You are, furthermore, using the fourth remedy, namely prayers and fasts, to appease the ire of God. This remedy would be very good and true, if the wrongs which I have mentioned did not prevent it from being effective. But there where cruelty and derision exist, fasts and prayers find no favour whatsoever with God. Solomon shows this clearly, when he says: "He that turneth away his ear from hearing the law, even his prayer shall be abomination."[7] And Isaiah puts this still more clearly, when he says that God speaks as follows to His people: "To what purpose is the multitude of your sacrifices unto me? saith the Lord: I am full of the burnt offerings of rams, and the fat of fed beasts; and I delight not in the blood of bullocks, or of lambs, or of goats. When ye come to appear before me, who hath required this at your hand, to tread my courts? Bring no more vain oblations; incense is an abomination unto me; the new moons and sabbaths, the calling of assemblies, I cannot away with; it is iniquity, even the solemn meeting. Your new moons and your appointed feasts my soul hateth: they are trouble unto me; I am weary to bear them. And when ye spread forth your hands, I will hide mine eyes from you: yea, when ye make many prayers, I will not hear: your hands are full of blood. Wash you, make you clean; put away the evil of your doings from before mine eyes; cease to do evil; learn to do well; seek judgment, relieve the oppressed, judge the fatherless, plead for the widow."

"Come now and let us reason together saith the Lord: though your sins be as scarlet, they shall be as white as snow; though they be red like crimson, they shall be as wool. If ye be willing and obedient, ye shall eat the good of the land: But if ye refuse and rebel, ye shall be devoured with the sword: for the mouth

---

[7] Prov. 28:9.

of the Lord hath spoken it. How is the faithful city become an harlot! It was full of judgment; righteousness lodged in it; but now murderers."[8] This is the word of the Lord, oh Evangelics, from which you can well understand that, though you may pray and fast as much as you like, the Lord will hide His eyes from you, unless you mend your ways. For, in truth, you cannot deny that your hands are full of blood, which fact is so very true indeed that one of your preachers, who was a Christian and of noble spirit, cried: "Must I preach here amongst murderers?" on seeing his listeners still blood-stained from the murders which they had just committed. And another, elsewhere, moved by a similar cause, said: "You fight against idolaters, as enemies of God, and do you think that God, who hates idolaters, likes murderers?"

Lest you say to me that it is true that your hands are full of blood, but that you have shed and spent it righteously, and in accordance with the will of God, I reply that even if this were so (which I do not avow, however), you still would but be God's executioners, sent to destroy the Church of the Antichrist (assuming that it could be destroyed by mortal arms) and not to build the one of Christ. For if David, however much he had acted in accordance with God's will, was not allowed to build the temple of God, a temple which was still material, because of the blood which he had shed and the wars which he had waged, I leave it to you to consider whether you will be permitted or charged to build the spiritual temple with your bloodied hands. Certainly not. It will have to be a Solomon, that is to say men of peace, who will build the temple of the Lord. It is therefore based on false principles that you wish to be considered reformers of the Church, and that you call your churches reformed Churches, whereas, judging by your actions, they should in fact be called destroying churches. And I have indeed heard it said

---

[8]   Isaiah 1:11–21.

that your predecessor, Martin Luther, once openly admitted it. When asked the reason why his people did not amend their lives, he replied that God had sent him to destroy the Pope and not to build the Church, and that He would afterwards send someone else to do the building. But Luther was much more reasonable than you, for he at least fought with his tongue and his pen, without taking up arms, and not forcing others to do so but, rather, dissuading them from it, as is evidenced by the book which he wrote about the magistracy.[9] And you did, as a matter of fact, once follow him, but now you are going very much further. Now I have said this on the supposition that that which you are doing is being done by you in accordance with God's will, which supposition I can, however, not grant you. And, so that you will hear me, I am now going to address my argument to both of you, for you are both in the same situation with regard to this matter.

To the Catholics and the Evangelics, Concerning the Forcing of One Another's Consciences

It is a fact that when Jesus Christ argued with the Jews, he sometimes, however much they might be obstinate, convinced them so thoroughly with a single utterance of obvious truth that they were left quite speechless, not answering a single word. This happened when he said to them: "Render therefore unto Caesar the things which be Caesar's and unto God the things which be God's."[10] And also: "He that is without sin among you, let him first cast a stone...."[11] I wish the world were no more obstinate today than those people. I am quite persuaded that the

---

[9]   Luther's Treatise "Von Weltlicher Oberkeit" (1523, WA XI, pp. 229 ff.)

[10] St. Luke 20:25.

[11] St. John 8:7.

matter which I am now discussing would then be resolved by a single utterance of obvious truth, and that there would then be no one who would dare to contradict, even in the slightest degree. For it would then but be necessary to say to those who force the consciences of others: "Would you like your own to be forced?" And their own conscience, which is worth more than a thousand witnesses, would then suddenly convince them so thoroughly, that they would be quite ashamed.

I would really like to take you up on these words and suppose that Jesus Christ ask you such a question (for the truth is also very much of Jesus Christ), would you, then, like your consciences to be forced? Answer in the name of Jesus Christ, answer me whether you would like your consciences to be forced. I am quite persuaded that your consciences answer no, and if this is the case, then why did you previously complain of the Catholics forcing yours, O Evangelics? And you, Catholics, why are you now beginning to complain of the Evangelics forcing yours? Are not your complaints condemning you, considering that you are doing those very things which you are finding fault with in others? Do you not know that Paul says: "Therefore thou art inexcusable, O man, whosoever thou art that judgest: for wherein thou judgest another, thou condemnest thyself…. Thou therefore which teachest another, teachest thou not thyself? Thou that preachest a man should not steal, dost thou steal?"[12] I ask you whether one cannot with the same reasoning say the following: "You are saying that one should not force consciences, but you are forcing those of others."

But do as you wish and seek everywhere in all diligence such scapegoats as you may, your own consciences will accuse you both at the day of Judgment, and in your own hearts will you carry your witnesses, witnesses which you will neither be able to despise nor reproach. And with you it will come to pass as

---

[12] Rom. 2:1 & 21.

with the Ephraimites of old, who were put to death by the Galaadites, because they were unable to pronounce the word Schibbolet, but pronounced it Sibbolet instead, from which pronunciation the Galaadites knew that they were Ephraimites. If you do not repent in time, you will thus be condemned at the judgment of the God of truth, for the reason that you will be unable to say that you have done to others as you would like others to do to you.

You should thus not excuse yourselves at this point, saying as a certain one once said: "If I were an adulterer, I would not like to be punished, but it does not follow from this, however, that if I were a judge, I should not punish an adulterer." For I would then answer as follows: "If you were an adulterer, and you were to be punished for it, you would have to admit that this would certainly not be an injustice." And a brigand or a thief, when punished, admits that he has indeed deserved it, or if he denies it with his mouth, his conscience will still contradict this and admit it in spite of himself. The invisible force of truth and righteousness which cannot be abolished from the heart of man, however evil he may be, is indeed clearly demonstrated through this. But this is not so with one whose conscience is forced, and who is persecuted because of his faith. For, however much one may force him to confess with his mouth that he is not being treated unjustly, his heart will still always say: "You are doing me an injustice, and you would not like this to be done to you." And this is how this rule should, in accordance with the truth, be understood. "Do not to another that which you would not like to be done to you." This is such a true, just and natural rule, so much written into the hearts of all men by the law of God, that no one, however perverted and far-removed from all discipline and teaching he may be, would fail to admit its righteousness and reasonableness, as soon as it is put to him, from which it is fair to deduce that when the truth will judge us, it will do so in accordance with this rule. And Christ, who is truth, in fact confirms this when He not only forbids us to do something to someone else which we would not like to be done to us, but, what is more, commands us to do that to others which we would like to be done to us.[13] He furthermore says that we shall be measured with the same measure with which we shall have measured others.[14]

At this point I could well end my argument, the matter being so obvious and so thoroughly inscribed into the conscience of everyone by the finger of God, that only a stubborn person or a fool might possibly contradict it. But as the same has been pointed out to you by the writings of certain others in the past, and as you have nevertheless persevered in your wrong ways, I now want to endeavor to draw you, finally, out of your stubbornness and to open your eyes somewhat, since you have both, for the same reason, come to suffer great anguish. It is generally said: "A fool only believes in as much as he receives." And Isaiah writes that only torment will cause his propositions to be heard. Listen at least now, whilst you are being so horribly tormented, and do not follow the Jewish zealots of the time of Vespasian and Titus, emperors of Rome, which zealots were, I would say, not so much zealots, but rather fanatics. For they preferred to die rather than to turn over a new leaf, and in so doing caused the Jewish nation to be afflicted with grave ills, which are still continuing today. It is said better later than never. At least make amends now, in case the God of mercy may perhaps take pity on you. I can, indeed, assuredly tell you that you may otherwise but expect ills without number and, in the end, a terrible punishment by God, who will render to each in accordance with his works.

Thus, to revert to my argument, I am now, in view of your hardheadedness, forced to examine the subject in somewhat

---

[13] Comp. St. Matthew 7:12.

[14] Comp. St. Matthew 7:2.

greater detail. I therefore ask you whether, when you thus force people's consciences, you are doing so by the commandment of God, by the example of certain holy persons, or by good intentions, thinking that you are doing well. For apart from these three points, I can see no reason for your doing it, unless, as I am inclined to believe, you are doing it out of pure malice.

About the Commandments of God

If you say that you are doing it in accordance with the commandments of God, I ask you where He has commanded it, for in the entire Bible I do not find a single word about it; even in the law of Moses which is otherwise rather rigorous, considering that in one place it goes so far as to command the murdering and massacring of the men, beasts and towns of idolaters, one nevertheless does not find a single word about one having to force consciences. It does, however, permit strangers to be received into the Israelite community if they are, of their own accord, prepared to be circumcised. But I find nothing written about one having to force them to do so. Indeed, those very ones who have written books urging the persecution and killing of heretics,[15] have been unable to quote a single passage to prove that one should force consciences, although they were quite diligent enough not to have forgotten it, would it have been possible to find one.

And certainly, if God had commanded the forcing of consciences, this would, firstly, have been contrary to nature, of which He, Himself, is the creator. And nature has, as mentioned above, so thoroughly impressed this rule, namely: "Do not to another something which you would not like to be done to you" into the heart of all nations, that no man, however perverted and far-removed from all doctrine he may be, can fail to admit

---

[15] An allusion to *De Haereticis* by Theodore de Bèze (1554).

that it is wrong to act against this rule. Secondly, it would be contrary to His own commandment, considering that He has commanded this very thing through Jesus Christ. Indeed, what is more, Saint Paul quite rigorously reprimands someone who, through his example in eating flesh, causes another to do likewise against his conscience, and comes to the following conclusion: "But when ye sin so against the brethren, and wound their weak conscience, ye sin against Christ."[16] Likewise, elsewhere: "All things indeed are pure; but it is evil for that man who eateth with offence. For meat destroy not the work of God."[17] And if he so earnestly reprimands him who, by his example, causes another to sin against his conscience, without forcing him in any other way, indeed, without even telling him to do it, what would he say today if he saw the enormous violations which you are doing to consciences not by example, but as much by words as by deeds, by censuring, condemning, vilifying, banishing, depriving of their honour, their possessions and often of their body, those who cannot in good conscience believe or do what you believe or do? For if that is not forcing, then I do not know what forcing is. It is, indeed, impossible to commit greater violence, and yet I really believe that if you could find a greater one, you would commit it.

Now consider in what sort of position you are placing these poor people. Here you have a man who has scruples about going to mass or about listening to the sermon of a preacher whom he considers to be a heretic, or about helping either with money or with his person and arms a Church which he considers heretical, against a Church which he considers catholic, and you tell him that he will be banished, disinherited or dishonourably put to death if he does not do it. What do you want him to do? Give him advice, for he is in extreme anguish, much like a slice of

---

[16] 1 Cor. 8:12.

[17] Rom. 14:20.

bread which is being toasted on a point of a knife, is burnt if it moves forwards and pricked if it moves backwards. Thus this poor man, in acting against his conscience, damns himself if he does as you want him to, and loses his possessions or his life, a weighty matter for every being, if he does not. What do you advise him here?

At least you, both old and new teachers and inquisitors of the faith, who are urging the princes to do this (for it is well known that it is you who are urging them, and I really do not think that you will deny it, considering that your actions and sermons and even your books are so obviously witnessing this), what advice do you give to such a man? Do you advise him to act against his conscience? His soul will perish. Do you recommend that he should act in accordance with his conscience? He will be put to death. The matter is such that he can indeed say what Susan said to those two old men who wanted to violate her: "I am anguished from all sides, for should I do it, I am dead, and should I refrain from it, I will also not escape from your hands."

And I know well what some used to say here: "We would gladly teach them, but they are stubborn and they always persevere with their own ideas, whatever one says to them." To which I reply: "But then, you propose things to them which would cause astonishment were they accepted by a man of good conscience and which, not surprisingly, they do not accept." But let us assume that you are propounding the truth to them (as I believe you occasionally do) and that they do not accept it, what could one do about it? Would you make them accept it by force? If a sick person could not eat the good food which you might offer to him, would you force it down his throat by force? Or if a donkey does not want to drink, would you drown it to make it drink? Learn from Christ, and follow His example. When He came into contact with stubborn people He left them and said to His disciples: "Leave them." And so much for the commandment.

Examples

As far as examples are concerned, I find that there has neither in the Old nor in the New Testament ever been a holy man—what, holy?—a man who forced or wanted to force consciences like you are doing. Moreover I will, in this respect, say that even if there were any who might have done it, one should not draw conclusions from it, nor follow their example, considering that they would have acted against all reason and against the commandment of God. For examples do not make the commandment, but the commandment makes the examples, and should one not follow an example only in so far as it is in accordance with, or at least not against, the commandment of God? When it becomes necessary to decide what we should do, we should always look at the commandment of God and act accordingly.

Otherwise one could find plenty of examples (not of the forcing of consciences, for of this, as said, I cannot find any, but of other relevant matters), which examples it would be more than dangerous to follow. Dangerous as it would be to follow the example of Moses, who killed an Egyptian without any form of process, and of Phineas who did the same with two sinners, and of Jacob who lied to his father, saying that he was Esau, and of the Israelites, who pillaged the Egyptians in accordance with a particular commandment of God, borrowing and carrying off their crockery; and of David, who, in the service of Achish, king of Gath, waged campaigns against the Geshurites and other enemies of the Israelites and butchered everybody, sparing not a man or a woman, and then gave his master Achish to understand that he had overrun the country of Judea.[18] And, again, of the same David, who, far from punishing the slanderer Siba, after he had become aware of his slander, even went so far as to reward him with half of his master's possessions, even

---

[18] Comp. 1 Sam. 27:8–11.

though, according to law, he should have punished and not rewarded him. These and other similar examples of holy men, whether the Scriptures in so many words approve of them, or whether they are there related without judgment being passed on them, should not, when they are considered, be taken as a rule, nor should conclusions be drawn from them, except as said.

Or else a dissolute person will find his excuse in Judas, who associated with Thamare, thinking that she was a whore, a drunkard in Lot and Noah, a liar in David, in the above example, and in Abraham who said that his wife was his sister, a cruel person in the above-mentioned David, who made the Ammonites go through a tile-baking furnace and tormented them with saws, harrows and steel axes. Such examples, briefly, are too dangerous to consider as matter for deliberation and have caused many to stumble. And with this it often happens as with a child, who wishes to act like a man who wields a sword and knows how to handle it, but hurts himself or another, because he is a child and does not know how to handle it. And furthermore, even if there were no danger, there are no examples concerning the forcing of consciences to be found, and even if there were, one should still not follow them, for the reasons set out above.

But the most important reason of all is that we owe allegiance to Christ, whose doctrine and example we have to follow, irrespective of what the others said or did, considering that the Father told us that He is His dear Son, and that we should listen to Him and obey Him.[19] It is this Son of God who forbade His disciples to follow Elias' example and to call down the fires of Heaven, telling them that they did not know of which spirit they were, and that He had not come to destroy men's lives, like Elias, but to save them.[20] It is this Son of God who told us that we would go after Him, and that all those who go before Him,

---

[19] Comp. St. Matthew 17:5.

[20] St. Luke 9:54, 55.

are thieves and robbers.[21] And go before Him is what those are doing who are forcing consciences without, and even against, His commandment and example. For they cannot say that they are going after Christ. They are going very much before Him, through which they are proving themselves to be thieves and robbers. It is this Christ who has given us a perfect law which we should regard with at least the same degree of reverence as the law of Moses. This means that we should be careful that we do not add to it, or take away from it, considering that the Father has, as said, commanded us to obey it. He also said that the nations should have confidence in His law. It is this Son of God who says to us: "Learn of me; for I am meek and lowly in heart: and ye shall find rest unto your souls."[22] If, therefore, we do not learn gentleness and humility from Him, let us not expect to find peace for our souls. And experience will indeed show you that people who thus force the consciences of others, never have peace in their hearts even in this life, let alone in the other. And so much for the examples from the Holy Scriptures.

And as far as other examples are concerned, not taken from the Holy Scriptures, I must admit that there have been some who have, in the past, forced consciences. One of these was Hyrcanus, pontiff of the Jews[23] after the time of the Maccabees, who forced the Idumenians to circumcise themselves. The same applies to those who once forced the Saracens to be baptised. And to those who, in Spain, forced the Jews to do the same. But, for the reasons given above, such people are no more to be followed than you. I do not even want to mention that their forcing had no better results than ours; for neither did the Saracens ever become true Christians, as they have since shown when they reverted to their former religion, nor were the Jews of Spain,

---

[21] St. John 10:7–8.

[22] St. Matthew 11:29.

[23] Josèphe, *Ant.*, lib. XIII, Cap. 9.

baptised by force, any more Christian than previously. They are, on the contrary, still preserving their old law and instructing their children in it, irrespective of what outward appearance they may, under duress, have to put up. It is for this reason that they are known by the infamous name Marrans, and one has in fact achieved nothing but the making of hypocrites and false Christians, through whom the name of Christ is blasphemed. I do not even wish to mention that even if some great benefit should result from such constraint, it would nonetheless still remain illicit, seeing that Saint Paul teaches that one should not do evil in order that good may result from it.

About the Good Intention

It but remains that what you are doing is being done by you as the result of a good intention, in the belief that you are doing well. But you know well, or you should at least know, that we must not follow our good intention, but the commandment of God, as He Himself says.[24] For one is sometimes seriously mistaken in thinking that one is doing well. This is evident from King Saul who had kept back the fattest beasts of the spoil to sacrifice them to God, and who was relieved of his reign for the reason that he had not done this because of the commandment of God, but only because of a good intention.[25] Likewise, from the words of Christ, who speaks as follows to his disciples: "They shall put you out of the synagogues: Yea, the time cometh, that whosoever killeth you will think that he doeth God service."[26] And if, in fact, your servants would do what might seem right to them, and not what you command them, you obviously would not be pleased about it. Do not think, therefore, that God is

---

[24] Comp. Deut. 12:32.

[25] 1 Sam. 15.

[26] St. John 16:2.

satisfied with your thinking that you are doing well, if it is not done in accordance with His commandment. But know that your servants will judge you at the day of Judgment, seeing that, by allowing them to think that they are doing well, they are doing what you command them, and that it is you who are acting against your master.

The Fruits of Forcing Consciences

Let us now consider the fruits which result from your constraint. Firstly, if those whom you are forcing, are strong and persevering and prefer to die rather than to hurt their consciences, you kill them, and as the murderers of their bodies you will have to answer to God for this. Secondly, if they are so weak that they prefer to go back on their word and hurt their consciences, rather than to endure your torments and insufferable tortures, you are causing their souls to perish, which is still worse. And for this you will have to render account to God, with whom they are, and be punished in accordance with the law of the like, which is: "With what measure ye mete, it shall be measured to you again."[27] Thirdly, you are causing enormous offence to all true Christians and children of God. These, having a spirit in Christ, who is the spirit of complete gentleness, goodness and kindness, are, not without cause, greatly offended by your enormous violence and are continuously wailing to God about it. And do not doubt that there are several amongst you who, fearing your violence, are effectively keeping quiet with their mouths, but whose heart cries to the Heavens, and whose cry reaches up to the ears of Him who hears the sighs of the wrongly oppressed. Now consider whether it is a small sin to offend so many God-fearing people, considering that Christ says that it would be much better to be thrown into the middle

[27] St. Matthew 7:2.

of the sea with a millstone around your neck than to give the least offence to those who believe in Him. Think awhile, I pray you, about this millstone. Fourthly, you are the reason why the holy name and holy and blessed doctrine of Jesus Christ is found fault with and blasphemed amidst foreign nations, like the Jews and Turks who, seeing such wars and carnages amongst the Christians, think that these are due to the doctrine, which they therefore curse and with which they are daily becoming more disgusted. Fifthly, you are the reason why enmities, hatred and mortal and immortal grudges are being engendered amongst you, which might perchance go from father to son, as much because of the violence caused to the living as because of the blood of the dead which has already been shed, the memory of which for a long time remains fresh in the hearts of their relatives and friends. These, now, are the great ills which result from your violence.

There is only one benefit which the less bad amongst you are perhaps hoping for as the reward for all these evils, namely that through such violence some will be gained for Christ. To which I firstly answer that even if this were so, this benefit could in no way be compared to so many such great disadvantages as have already been mentioned. Furthermore, for you to commit so many wrongs for such a benefit, is just as great a madness as for someone to sow a hundred barrels of corn in order to harvest one, or for someone to burn his house in order to obtain ashes, or for one to kill a hundred men already advanced in age, in order to beget a child. But supposing that the good which follows from it were not only equal to the wrong, but incomparably greater, one should still not do it, considering that, as already said, the truth teaches us that one should not do wrong in order that good may result from it.

And what will we say if the good which you are seeking in it is not there? You want to make Christians by force, and so doing honour God, but you are greatly deluding yourselves in this, for if that could or should be done, Christ would have been the very first to have done and instructed it, seeing that He has been sent to honour God and to cause God to be honoured, and that, to do this, He has the spirit of complete wisdom. But He acts quite differently, for He only wants voluntary disciples, without constraint, as symbolized and predicted in the Old Testament. Symbolised, in that the Tabernacle was made of gifts offered voluntarily by the people, and also in that God, when He teaches the people of Israel how to wage war, draws up a law for them to the effect that they shall, before entering into battle, make it known to all that he who is fearful, newly married, has built a new house or planted vines, should retire from the battlefield and return home, lest he cause others to lose courage in the battle. So much for the symbol. As far as the prediction is concerned, it appears in the Book of Psalms, there where God speaks the following words to Christ: "Thy people shall be willing in the day of thy power, in the beauties of holiness."[28] These are the true soldiers of Christ, voluntary, cheerful and regretting nothing whatsoever worldly. And those who make or want to make soldiers by force, certainly neither understand corporal nor spiritual war, but, instead of making real champions of Christ, they make cowards, fearful, shamming and effeminate people, who are of greater advantage to the enemy than to Christ.

I say this with full conviction and without any doubt, for I know that it is definitely so, and have the experience which will not let me lie, as proof. For we manifestly see that those who are forced to accept the Christian religion, whether they are a people or individuals, never make good Christians. And I fear that they will be even less so than before, for they are disgusted by such constraint, sometimes even to the point where they plug their ears for fear that they might hear what is being

---

[28] Psalm 110:3.

preached to them, and where they pray to God that He will grant them the grace to let them leave the sermon in the same condition as they came to it. If someone, thus forced, comes to believe (which I strongly doubt, however), but if he does come to believe, it does not happen as the result of the constraint. If he had perhaps not been forced, he would have believed as soon or sooner than he has, for we see that there where none are forced, the number of believers generally grows more than there where constraint exists. I could quote many examples of this, were these not already well-known to several, and did I not fear that some might be offended by them.

This is why I say that those who thus look to numbers and for that reason force people, gain nothing, but rather lose. They are like the fool who, possessing a large vat containing a small quantity of wine, fills it completely with water in order to have more, and so doing not only fails to increase his wine, but even spoils the good he had. Thus, such people wishing to augment the number of Christians, not only completely fail to do so, but even spoil whatever good there was. For this reason one should not be surprised that the wine of Christ is so minimal and so weak these days, considering that so much water is mixed with it. The Apostles did not act in this manner. They knew and adhered to the true way of making and receiving a Christian. Thus they rather asked the novice whether he believed, as Philip did with Queen Candace's eunuch: "If you believe with all your heart, you may be baptised." But you who force consciences could not ask your novices this. For when you force someone to acknowledge the power of the Pope, mass or purgatory, or the doctrine or ceremonies which you observe, through fear of dishonour or the loss of possessions or life, it is already no longer necessary for you to ask him whether he believes with all his heart, that is to say truthfully and without any doubt. For you should know (if you are not more blind than moles) that, very far from believing with all his heart, he, on the contrary, disbelieves with all his heart. If he dared to say what his heart believes and thinks, he would say: "I believe with all my heart that you are proper tyrants and that that which you are forcing me into, is worthless; so much so, indeed, that if I had had some inclination towards it before, you have now deprived me of it, as the result of your coercion." For it must be said that wine is worth but little if people are forced to drink it, and it must equally be said that your doctrine is worth but little if you have to force it onto people.

In short, you are acting like your predecessors in the olden days, when they seized Burgundy and forced the inhabitants to say: "Long live the King." For the latter rather let themselves be killed than to say: "Long live the King." Or, if someone through fear said it with his mouth, his heart said exactly the opposite, and hated the king even more than ever. Those whom you are forcing are doing the same, so much so, that you are but engendering mortal hatreds, and making deceiving and hypocritical Christians who afterwards think of and strive for nothing but the destruction of that into which they have been forced. They also teach their children this and revolt at the first opportunity which presents itself to them.

These are the evils which, instead of good, result from your good intentions and coercions. It is amazing if you do not see these and fail to notice that, instead of advancing your religion, you are even retarding it. Consider the matter well, so that you may realize that this is so. Firstly, when Luther began to make himself heard, you, Catholics, began to persecute his sect and to burn its members in order to suppress it, and you have since never ceased to endeavour, in every possible manner, to uproot it. And what have you gained? You have rendered yourselves suspect and have caused people to want to investigate what it was, as the result of which the matter became so important that a hundred have come in the place of the one which you have burned. The result is that there are more thousands of them today than there were dozens of them previously, so much so that, as you see, they already dare to make war against you.

It is the same with you, Evangelics. When, hitherto, you fought with spiritual arms, which you learnt and took from Christ and His Apostles, namely faith, love, patience and others, God blessed you and strengthened you so much that your cause always progressed from good to better and that your numbers grew manifold, like the dewdrops of the dawn of day. But now that you have abandoned spiritual arms and taken up mortal ones, everything is going completely awry for you. For your violence renders you suspect and causes people to regard you in a very bad light and to withdraw instead of stepping forward. So that you may understand that this is not a matter of chance, but great wisdom and the will of God, who generally from such causes makes such results come forth, you should understand that that which is happening to you has even, to your recollection, happened to others, namely to Zwingle and the Emperor Charles the Fifth. For while Zwingle fought with doctrine and words, his cause advanced so much that the whole country of Switzerland was moved to receive his doctrine. But when he came to use violence and himself put his hand to the sword, everything went awry, so much so that he himself and several others fell in battle and that the Catholic cantons which had previously accepted the doctrine, withdrew and confirmed their ancient faith to such a degree, even, that they have since never deviated from it.[29]

The same happened to the Emperor Charles. You know how he waged war against the Protestants and how he achieved a total victory, to the point even where he took and, for a long time, held their princes as prisoners. One might therefore have

---

[29] An allusion to the two wars of Kappel, where Zwingle led his compatriots from Zurich into battle against the Catholic cantons of central Switzerland, and where he met his death on the 11th October, 1531.

thought that their doctrine and religion were done with. But what finally happened? He was forced not by the Protestants, but by those very ones who had helped him and especially by your own King, O French, who was a mortal enemy of the Protestants' doctrine, to set the prisoners free. And their Protestant religion remained so complete, thanks to the assistance of its very enemies, that it still exists there today.[30] It seems that the God of armies clearly shows through such examples that He does not want these aims to be achieved through violence.

Consideration of the Future

Let us now consider what is likely to result from it, should you both persevere with your undertaking. As far as I can understand by studying the whole matter in detail, the war must, of necessity, either last indefinitely, or the one party will by force be persuaded and drawn to the religion of the other, or it will, out of fear, pretend to be drawn without being persuaded, or it will be completely annihilated by the other, or at least driven out of the country or, whilst remaining in the country, it will be miserably tyrannised, or the two parties will be overcome and subjugated by some enemy or enemies from outside, or they will make peace with one another on the condition that each will, without offending the other, without fear be able to follow whichever of the religions it desires. These are, it seems to me, the seven points of which one must come about, and concerning which one must take council and seek advice.

---

[30] The Protestant princes, in forming the Smalkade alliance, aided by Henry II, had obtained the confessional division of Germany from Charles the Fifth on the occasion of the Peace of Passau, in 1552.

The First Point

Let us now consider all seven and choose the best. The first, namely perpetual war, is wretched and detestable and should, as such, be avoided. I do not wish to mention that it is apparently impossible, considering that your war, unlike is usually the case, is an obstinate war tending towards the total destruction of the opposing party, considering that the one side as much as the other (as we see from your published protestations) has promised and assured that they would to this end use even the last cent of their purse and their last drop of blood. Would now to God (if I may say this in passing) that you had rather sworn by the image of Christ, and that you would use all your possessions and never cease until you had killed your old self and been recreated in the new one, and that, in loving your enemies, you would be like our celestial Father. That, yes, that now would be a holy and praiseworthy decision, a holy oath similar to the one which David took. David, namely, took an oath and swore to God that he would not go into his house or lie down on his bed or let his eyes sleep and rest, until he had found a place and a house for the God of Jacob. But this can I but wish for, for your actions prevent me from hoping for it. Thus, like an extremely serious illness cannot for long endure in a man without it either being cured or carrying him away, so also your war, it seems to me, cannot be perpetual. It will, therefore, either have to finish, or France will be destroyed.

The Second Point

As far as the second point is concerned, it is neither permissible nor possible. For to think that a conscience can be persuaded by force, is just such folly as for one to want to kill the thoughts of a man with a sword or a halberd.

The Third Point

The third point, which is to have deceitful people, who through fear pretend to be in agreement with the religion, but detest it in their heart, is quite the same as if a community wanted to have deceitful citizens who, whilst promising their loyalty with their mouths, hated the community in their hearts. Such a community would deserve to have traitors, instead of citizens. Alternatively, it is like a man desiring to have a wife who promised him faith of marriage with her mouth, but felt quite the opposite in her heart. Such a man would certainly deserve to have a secret wanton, instead of a loyal spouse.

The Fourth and Fifth Points

The fourth point, which is that one side be annihilated by the other or at least driven out of the country and, likewise, the fifth point, which is to tyrannise, no more resemble Christianity than a wolf resembles a sheep. If you do wish to do these things, you should rather entirely renounce the name of Christ and quite openly behave as the heathens and tyrants which you, in fact, are, since you are, in reality, in no way acquainted with the benign nature of Christ. You know what Elias said to the people of Israel: "How long halt ye between two opinions? if the Lord be God, follow him: but if Baal, then follow him."[31] Thus it will quite rightfully be said to you. If you are Christians, why do you use tyranny? If you are not Christians, why do you carry the name and, denying Christ by your actions, confess Him with your mouth? Do you know that Christ says: "Learn from me kindness and humility of heart."[32]

---

[31] 1 Kings 18:21.

[32] Comp. St. Matthew 11:29.

The Sixth Point

As far as the sixth point is concerned, it is wretched, and unless you are completely devoid of sense, I do not think that you desire it.

The Seventh Point

There now remains the seventh point, which is to settle the difference and to allow the two religions to remain free. If you do not accept this point, you will, of necessity, fall into one of the six disadvantages related hereabove. If all six are wretched or against God (as they certainly are, as we have shown), and if you wish (as you certainly should) to avoid misfortune as well as sin, it but remains for you to accept the seventh, which I say (and hope) will prove to be both without any sin and the great disadvantages of the others. But before coming to this point, I want to make mention of a small book, printed in French last year, entitled *Exhortation aux princes et seigneurs du conseil privé du Roy*.[33] In this book the same advice is given that I want to give, namely that two churches be permitted in France. The said book (in my opinion and in the opinion of all those who have read it and to whom I have spoken about it) has been written by a cautious man, whoever he may be, who gives very good and profitable advice. And, indeed, even the most unreasonable individuals will be forced to admit to me that, had he been followed, the death of at least fifty thousand Frenchmen, who have since been miserably murdered, would until now (not to make mention of the future) have been avoided. This would have been a benefit the importance of which it is now (after the

---

[33] "Exhortation to the princes and lords of the privy council of the King," an anonymous work by Etienne Pasquier, a Catholic partisan of the moderation movement.

benefit has been lost) easier to appreciate, than it would have been possible to forsee, had the misfortune not come about. For it is a fact that fools only appreciate the good after they have been deprived of it.

Well then, since one has until now, by refusing such good and moderate council and following a bad and bloody one, fallen into such great and irreparable evils, I have come to think that you will never learn or you would, like the fools, at least have learnt something this time. You have, until now, followed the advice of the most pitiless of your masters and teachers (it generally happens that one rather believes the bad than the good), and the results have been extremely unfortunate for you, not to mention that you have greatly offended Him, who is now, from up there, punishing you. Try another way now, and do as one does in the case of illnesses, where, each time one is dissatisfied with a doctor, one seeks another. Or do as Pharaoh, the King of Egypt, did in the olden days. When he failed to obtain any interpretation of his dreams from his magicians, he eventually summoned the poor and despised prisoner, Joseph, from whom he learnt what he sought, and whose advice he followed, with excellent results. You, who have until now been led astray by those who are leading you, should thus seek everywhere, to ascertain whether better guidance could not be found. Also, you should not be hardheaded, like the Alchemists who prefer to dispense with all their possessions, their being and their reason and finally either to die whilst blowing the coals, or to go and die in hospital, rather than to give up their senseless undertaking. Or like the gamblers, who prefer to play until they only have their shirt left, rather than to retain at least their leather jerkin. Or as the Jews did in the time of the Emperor Vespasian and his son Titus, when they preferred to watch their wonder, Jerusalem, with all of Judea and the Judaic nation fall into ashes and blood, rather than to let themselves be dissuaded from their foolhardy stubbornness.

Well, to come back to my argument, examine the said booklet and advice well, and you will find that you cannot do better than to follow it. And I could indeed well end my argument here and refer you to the said booklet, doing as counsellors sometimes do whilst holding counsel, when for the sake of brevity they say: "I stand by what so and so has said about it." But I see a difficulty here which must, if possible, be overcome, namely that there are some who teach and have taught, as much by words as by books, that it is the function of princes and lords of the judiciary to put heretics to death, and that they are acting against God, and will be punished, if they do not do this. This teaching is the principal cause of the carnages and butcheries which are taking place for the sake of religion today, and as long as it remains, and the princes believe in it, I see no remedy for the situation. For, as Christianity is today divided into so many sects, which all regard one another as heretics, it is impossible for the princes who believe in this doctrine of persecution, not to persecute and massacre those whom they regard as heretics.

But the crowning misfortune in this matter is the fact that those very ones who conceived and published this doctrine, are themselves regarded as heretics by all the other sects, and for that reason persecuted and massacred. In truth, they were already heretics when they put forth such a doctrine.[34] And, what is more, they hate and have hated and persecuted and tried to put to death those who have dared to contradict them in this opinion. It seems to me that in this they resemble the Jews, who (according to what Pliny tells us) did their very best to eradicate and destroy the small tree which carried the balm, because the Romans were protecting it to prevent its being spoilt; to the point that the Jews themselves were worse enemies of

[34] Without doubt an allusion to Calvin and Beze, who had given the magistrates of Geneva the theoretical justification for the condemnation of Servet.

their own possessions and life than their enemies, that is to say the Romans.

The people here are acting quite similarly, in that they hate and persecute those very ones who, by giving them instructions and advice, saved their lives. I take them as their own witnesses to prove that this is so. Is it not true that if one followed the advice of those who counsel against persecution, those very ones who instruct persecution would be spared and not persecuted, there where they are now themselves persecuted and beaten with their own stick, because their doctrine of persecution is being followed, to the degree, indeed, where one can say of them what Pliny said of the Jews, namely that they are fighting against their own lives. To come to the point now, the question is whether one should put heretics to death; and this question has been disputed and books have been written about it these past years, some avowing yes, and others no.[35] And since, when the world judges, the worse party often overcomes the better one, those who have said yes have gained the upper hand in the matter and convinced several others. Several have died as the result of this, both of their own people, and others, who were held for heretics and who would certainly not have been put to death, had the opposite opinion been accepted.

Now, since the persecuting opinion is contrary to our advice and endeavour, and as the princes are unwilling not to persecute, it would be well to refute it and prove it erroneous. But because they who have hitherto written about it, have (it seems to me) done so adequately, were it not for the very great obstinacy of people, and as I should, for the moment, not be too long, I shall refer to what they have written about it without otherwise following the text in detail. I shall therefore only stop at two points which I have touched upon hereabove, namely to show that one

---

[35] Particularly those which Castellio wrote in support of the *no*, and the one which Beze wrote in support of the *yes*. (See Introduction.)

can safely refrain from persecuting those whom one holds for heretics and let them live, and that there is neither such great sin nor disadvantage in this, as there is in doing otherwise; and that if one should choose the lesser of two evils, as one certainly should, one should choose this one.

What a Heretic Is

Hence, so as to make myself understood, I would like to demonstrate simply, in few words, and in accordance with the truth, what a heretic is. The word *heretic* is a Greek word, derived from the word *heresy*, which means "sect." In this way a *heretic* is really one who belongs to a sect, such as existed, in the past, amongst the Philosophers, Academics, Peripatetics, Stoics, Epicureans and, in Judea, the Pharisees, Sadducees, Essenes, Nazarenes and Rechabites, and as would today be all sects of people who call themselves Christians, such as the Romans, Greeks, Georgians, Lutherans, Zwinglians, Waldenses, Picardians, Anabaptists and others and, amongst the Romans, the groups of monks which are called orders, such as the Franciscans, Augustinians, Carthusians and others. All such groups of people are, in accordance with the Greek word and in the manner of speaking of the Scriptures, called *heresies*, and those who belong to them, *heretics*. But when they are being referred to in an unfavourable manner, the word *heresy* is understood to mean "bad sect" and *heretic* one who belongs to a bad sect, much as in French, when one talks of a *garse*[36] in an unfavourable manner, one visualizes an unchaste woman, a whore, in other words, whereas the word *garse* in actual fact means girl. A *heretic*, therefore, is one who belongs to a bad sect. All this I could easily prove. But as it is obvious to all who know Greek and the Scriptures, I shall take it as completely proved and admitted.

---

[36] Young woman.

Whether One Should Put Heretics to Death

Now the question is whether one should put heretics to death, and whether the princes and lords of the judiciary would be acting wrongly, should they not put them to death. To which I answer no, for the reason that God has never commanded it, either in the Old or in the New Testament. For this I take as witnesses those very ones who wrote books with the express purpose of demonstrating that one should kill heretics and who, searching in all diligence for all passages through which it might be possible to prove their argument, have never been able to find one, in the entire Scriptures, wherein it is commanded that heretics should be put to death. Seeing this, and nevertheless wishing to maintain their opinion, they proceeded to prove that God had commanded in the Old Testament that blasphemers and false prophets should be put to death, and on the strength of this they concluded that one should therefore kill heretics as blasphemers and false prophets. If they could prove that heretics are such blasphemers and false prophets as are those whom Moses commands should be killed, I would indeed admit that Moses had commanded the killing of heretics and I would then not argue about the text, as we would be in agreement about the matter. But this is not the case. For, when Moses commands that a blasphemer should be put to death, he speaks of one who out of spite and knowingly, comes to blaspheme the name of God, as we see many gamblers do, and also old soldiers, drunkards and others. And that this is so, becomes clear as much through Moses' example as through his commandment. For it is there narrated how a dispute arose between one who was the son of an Israelite woman and an Egyptian father, who blasphemed and cursed the name of God, and an Israelite.[37] For which reason the Lord commanded that

---

[37] Comp. Levit. 24:10–13.

he should be stoned, and made a law about it, of which the words are as follows: "Whosoever curseth his God shall bear his sin" and "he that blasphemeth the name of the Lord, he shall surely be put to death."[38] Here we clearly see that he speaks of the curses and profanities which are generally called blasphemies and which are very well understood, even by the humbler classes. For even the impious communities have laws about it and generally punish such blasphemies.

But to apply this law to heretics, who might badly understand and expose some point in the Scriptures, such as the Holy Communion or baptism and others, and to say that they should, under this law, be put to death, is to cite wrongly and dangerously, and to be too cunningly keen to shed blood. One might as well say that under the same law the Sadducees should have been put to death because they denied the resurrection of the dead; or the Jewish Christians because they maintained that one had to be circumcised in order to be saved; or Paul, because he had, before becoming a Christian, in ignorance blasphemed Christ and His sect; or Thomas, because he denied the resurrection of Jesus Christ, even though he had the Scriptures, the prophecy of Christ and the witness of His apostles in evidence of it.

Likewise, it is certain that, as far as false prophets are concerned, he definitely is not referring to a heretic. This is clear from his words which are as follows: "If there arise among you a prophet, or a dreamer of dreams, and giveth thee a sign or a wonder, and the sign or the wonder come to pass, whereof he spake unto thee, saying, 'Let us go after other gods, which thou hast not known, and let us serve them;' thou shalt not hearken unto the words of that prophet ... and that prophet or that dreamer of dreams, shall be put to death."[39] These are the words of the law of Moses, from which it is evident that, in order to

---

[38] Levit. 24:15–16.
[39] Deut. 13:1–3, 5.

put a man to death under this law, three things are necessary: Firstly that the said prophet or dreamer of dreams foretells some sign or miracle; secondly that the said sign or miracle comes about; and thirdly that the said prophet or dreamer of dreams urges the people to adore other gods. If all three of these points do not exist, even though one or two may exist, one cannot kill a man in accordance with this law. Now it is a fact that in heretics, or in those who are regarded as heretics, not only these three points do not exist, but not even one of them, for which reason one cannot put them to death in accordance with this law.

I fully understand that someone will say (as some have dared to write) that, since the heretics falsify the Scriptures and teach that God is different from what He is, it is the same as if they were urging the adoration of other gods, since they teach that God is different from what He is. But without their blessing I reply that they are too cunningly keen to shed blood. Furthermore this is like someone saying that those who, at the time of the apostles, believed and said that Christ had come to save only the Jews, and who were consequently offended because Peter had gone to teach Cornelius, a heathen centurion, made God out to be other than what He is, namely as the saviour of only the Jews and not of heathens and that, consequently, they were idolaters. One must not, where a matter of such great importance as that of putting a man to death is concerned, in this manner proceed to distort and set forth the law as one pleases, but one must squarely, without exaggerating or minimizing the crime, confine oneself to the words and intentions of the law. Saint Paul indeed calls avarice idolatry, because a miser makes a god of his money. Must one, however, conclude that a miser should be put to death in accordance with the law which commands that idolaters should be killed? He also writes against those who make a god of their stomach. Must one consequently conclude that a magistrate should condemn a glutton or a drunkard to death as an idolater?

Those are the principal and most obvious arguments taken from the Scriptures, held by those who want heretics to be killed, and those arguments having been refuted, all the others are easy to reject and, with the aid of the truth, I hope to be able to do so. But I refrain from doing so for the moment, for fear of being too lengthy and having regard for your danger and misfortune, O France. You are more in need of brief advice than a long discourse. Since God has neither in the Old nor in the New Testament commanded the killing of heretics, and since we may neither take away from, nor add to His law and commandments, and since, for this reason, He will punish not only those who failed to do what He commanded, but also those who did that which He had not commanded, I say in conclusion that one should certainly not kill them and that, at the very worst, the magistrate will always have a just excuse for not having killed them by saying: "Lord, you certainly did not command us to do it." If, on the contrary, he does kill them, at the very best he could always, with justification, be reprimanded by God, speaking as follows: "I definitely did not command you to do it." In fact, if the princes were wise, they would speak as follows to the theologians when these incite them to put heretics to death: "Show us a divine law which expressly commands it," and then all the theologians in the world would not know what to say. When God proscribes the functions of a king, He commands that he should have a copy of the law in a book and that he should retain this and read it every day of his life, without deviating from it either to the right, or to the left.[40]

Remember this, O Princes, and do not trust so much in your counsellors, unless you have specific words of God's commandment, before putting your hand to the sword, for you are in a position where it will be necessary for you to very much render account of yourselves. One should not seek an excuse, saying

---

[40] Deut. 17:18–19.

that in Moses' time God made no commandment about heretics because there were, at that time, no heretics, for I answer that God did indeed know the future and that He made His commandments both for the present and for the future, indeed more for the future than for the present, considering that He told them that He was giving them the commandments to keep for when they would arrive in the promised land. At the time of Moses there was not a king in Israel, indeed God did not want there to be one. Even so, He does not fail to give them instructions for the king to come, as we have now proved. I say the same in respect of homosexuals, people who would have sexual intercourse with animals, dowsers, charmers and soothsayers, and as has been demonstrated hereabove, false prophets and others, all of which different kinds of people did not exist amongst the Israelites at that time. Yet God did not fail to provide them with laws about this for the future. For God is a perfect God, and gives a perfect law, and for that reason He forbids adding to it, or taking away from it. Those who add to it or take away from it, and raise scruples with men there where God does not do so, want to be greater and more perfect than God is in His works and commandments; and about this they will, in the end, have to render a far greater account than they think.

I am now going to reply lengthily to those who, fearing that they might not otherwise succeed in persuading the princes to put heretics to death, have dared to write that heretics sin against their consciences, however much they might deny this, while being obstinate to the death. For since such people are so brazen as to put themselves in the place of God, namely by judging the hearts of men without regard for their achievements, but rather by taking note of contrary achievements and as it is a fact that Christ taught us only to judge the tree by its fruit, I will leave them to the just judge, who will certainly know how to remeasure them with the same measure. Indeed, if someone said of them that they had pronounced such a sentence against their conscience, however much they might deny it, being obstinate even to the death, he would be doing nothing to them that they themselves had not already done to others.

So much for the first point, which is that the princes can, without sinning, let the heretics live; even if they should fall under the law of Moses, seeing that Moses did not make a single commandment about it. If under Moses himself, who gave such a strict law, it is definitely not commanded that a heretic should be killed, and if during all the time of the Law, that is to say from Moses until Christ, it is found that one has at no time killed a man for heresy, consider, then, what the law should be under Christ, and whether it would be right that the Law which must end, and ends, under Christ, should now in the first instance be executed under Christ, even though it has never been applied previously. For, so that you may understand this, we are not under Moses, but under Christ, so much so that even if Moses had commanded it, it would not necessarily follow from this that those who are under Christ should for this reason adhere to it. Or else we should become Jews and let ourselves be circumcised and follow the entire law. Even those very ones who have written books urging persecution, and who have been so industrious that they have searched for everything possible from the creation of the world up till their time, are nevertheless forced to admit that we are not at all subject to the law of Moses.

They would even, I believe, no longer dare to say that we are subject to the Law regarding the killing of idolaters with which they so strongly arm themselves, considering that it commands the massacring, by the edge of the sword, of a town in which there would be idolaters, the town and its livestock and everything in it, and the assembly of the entire booty in the centre of the town square, and the putting to the torch of the entire town and its booty, whilst nothing of this massacre should besmirch their hands.[41] This is the law for the punish-ment of idolaters, and if they want to apply it to heretics, I am indeed amazed about it, and I dare say that they are then very far removed from the spirit of Christ, considering that this law spares neither animals nor children.

If they say that they want to follow a part of it and not the rest, they will be asked who has granted them the privilege to divide a law in two parts, and whether it is not playing and trifling with the law of God, to take for their advantage that which pleases them, and to leave the rest. If they say that it is not because of its authority that they want to follow the law of Moses, that is to say, even though it is the law of Moses, but because of reason, and that they do not want a heretic to be killed, even though Moses has commanded that a false prophet or an idolater should be killed, but because there is as much reason for putting a heretic to death as a false prophet or an idolater, I will answer them that in so far as they say that one should follow reason, they are right, and we agree with them. But in so far as they hold the view that there is just as much reason to kill a heretic as a false prophet or an idolater, several men of reason do not agree with them.

On this point they advance their reasons for, and others their reasons against, and much argument has taken place about this difference of opinion on both sides, as much by books as by words. What to do, since we cannot agree which reasons are better? What to do since, in belonging to the differing parties ourselves, we cannot also be the judges? Who will judge the matter? For one must either postpone the pronounciation of judgment until such time as the dispute has been resolved, or have a capable judge, who judges with authority. We are in agreement with the postponement of judgment and quote the

---

[41] Deut. 13:12–16.

very reasonable law of credences[42] in this connection, but the persecutors do not agree to it. Let us therefore go to the judge and let us, by reason, follow the commandment of God regarding this point. This is found in Deuteronomy, there where He commands as follows: "If there arise a matter too hard for thee in judgment …, then shalt thou arise, and get thee up into the place which the Lord thy God shall choose: And thou shalt come unto the priests the Levites, and unto the judge that shall be in those days, and enquire; and they shall shew thee the sentence of judgment: According to the sentence of the law which they shall teach thee, and according to the judgment which they shall tell thee, thou shalt do: thou shalt not decline from the sentence which they shall shew thee, to the right hand, nor to the left. And the man that will do presumptuously, and will not hearken unto the priest, that standeth to minister there before the Lord thy God, or unto the judge, even that man shall die: and thou shalt put away the evil from Israel."[43] Likewise, a little further: "The Lord thy God will raise up unto thee a Prophet from the midst of thee, of thy brethren, like unto me; unto him ye shall hearken."[44] And a little further: "I will raise them up a Prophet from among their brethren, like unto thee, and will put my words in his mouth; and he shall speak unto them all that I shall command him. And it shall come to pass that whosoever will not hearken unto my words which he shall speak in my name, I will require it of him."[45]

There you have the ordinance of the Lord, concerning disputes which are difficult to judge. Now the place of which He speaks and which He had to choose, was, thereafter, the city

---

[42] The custom of the inhabitants of Normandy, by which witnesses established whether a matter was, or was not as alleged.

[43] Deut. 17:8–12.

[44] Deut. 18:15.

[45] Deut. 18:18–19.

of Jerusalem, where one had to go and see the High Priest or Pontiff, for the settlement of any disputes which might have arisen. But now that we are neither Israelites in the flesh, nor subject to the law of Moses in the flesh, and that we have neither Jerusalem nor the Pontiff, nor the High Priest in the flesh, we must address ourselves to the heavenly and spiritual Jerusalem, namely the church, and to the heavenly Pontiff, namely Christ, with our differences, as is evidenced by the chapter in Hebrews.[46] Also, we should address ourselves to the prophet of whom Moses speaks, who is the same Christ, as is evidenced by St. Stephen[47] and act in accordance with His judgment, on pain of God's indignation. And as Christ is no longer on this earth in person (for if He were, one would have to go and look for Him), and as we find ourselves in a period of famine with regard to God's word, that is to say a period without prophets and oracles (for if there were any, it would but be necessary to go to them, and the difference would be resolved), I can find no way to ascertain His judgment, except from His written words, or from the example of His life, or from the nature of His Spirit, as manifested in His followers, or by some new revelation.

As far as His written word is concerned, it definitely does not say that one should kill a heretic. It does, however, say in general that if someone sins (which applies as much to a heretic as to someone else), he should be several times legitimately admonished and finally excommunicated, if he does not make amends, which duty belongs to the church and not to the magistrate. It particularly stresses that a heretic should be avoided after he has been admonished once or twice. But it says nothing about killing him. Now it is a fact that Moses says that the said prophet (who is Christ, as has been proved

---

[46] Hebr. 7–8, 9:11 & foll.

[47] Acts 7.

hereabove), will say whatever God shall have commanded Him to say. Even so, Christ definitely does not say that one should kill heretics, and God has therefore not commanded Him to say it. Or, at least, we find nothing in the Scriptures about it, and if we do not hold ourselves to and believe in these, I really think that we would not believe in Him either, should He speak to us in person. Similarly Abraham told Dives that if his brothers did not believe in Moses and the prophets, that is to say in their writings, they would not even believe in a resuscitated person either.

As far as the life of Christ is concerned, we see it to have been so noble, that to seek the example for the killing of a heretic by the sword in it, would be very much like seeking the example for the eating of a wolf, in a lamb. As far as His spirit, which in manifested in His followers is concerned, His disciples are such that they follow the Lamb wherever it goes, and that they have learned from Him who is noble and humble of heart. If someone does not have this spirit, though he may call himself a Christian as much as he likes, he is just as far from Christ as darkness is from light. And the persecutors themselves, indeed, finding nothing but complete gentleness in the New Testament, entirely contrary to their persecution, are forced to take recourse to the Old Testament, through which they clearly show that they do not know of which spirit they are, and that they do not possess the spirit of the new alliance.

As to the new revelation, those very ones who instruct the persecution of heretics, do not claim to have it, and if they did, one would have to think twice before believing it, considering that it would be contrary to the perfection both of the law of Moses and the law of Christ. For which reason, since neither Moses nor Christ commanded the killing of a heretic, I say in conclusion that the magistrate can, with a clear conscience, and without offending God, let him live, and speak as follows to the theologians who are urging him to kill him: "Show us the law under which God has commanded you to do it, and we shall do it."

Here, now, we must take note of a point which has been touched upon in the above-cited law, namely that he who does not obey the said pontiff, shall, in accordance with the said law, be put to death. Now it is a fact that the debauched, quarrelsome, drunkards and the like, who have heard the doctrine of Christ and nevertheless persevere with their dark works, are disobeying Christ; from which it follows that they should, in accordance with the said law, be put to death. If someone retorts that the said law only speaks of those who might disobey Him in the matter of disputes which they might have amongst each other, I shall answer him that if a man must die for disobedience in the matter of a dispute, he should do so all the more for disobedience in a graver matter. But let us suppose that the law only speaks of disputes. At the very least it will follow from this that he who hates his brother and does not forgive and love him, and he who does not reconcile himself with his adversary whilst he is still on the way, that is to say prior to coming before the judgment of God, should die in accordance with this law. From this again it will follow that all those who do an injustice to another and are, as such, in dispute with another, and do not want to reconcile themselves with the other, shall, in accordance with the doctrine of the High Priest Christ, be put to death. From this it will follow that whoever does not want to reconcile himself with God (which reconciliation cannot take place unless man renounces the works of the flesh), shall be put to death. From this it will, consequently, follow that all those who live according to the flesh, shall be put to death. And still, no one will fail to admit to me that one cannot kill a man for avarice, or drunkenness, or ambition, or quarrelling and other sins of that kind. And yet one disobeys the High Priest Christ when committing such sins, from which it follows that the death from which such disobedients will die, has to be other than corporal.

It should, namely, be a spiritual death, in as much as Christ is not the corporal, but the spiritual Pontiff. This so much so that, however much a man may quite flatly deny Christ and disobey His words (as all those do who lead a dissipated life who, confessing Him by mouth, deny Him with their actions, which are obvious and need no witnesses), he nevertheless should decidedly not be put to death by the magistrate (I except civil cases, which deserve hanging), but is, rather, reserved for eternal death. Of such a death and punishment spoke Christ when, sending His disciples out to preach, He said to them that whoever would not receive them would be more harshly dealt with on the Day of Judgment than those of Sodom and Gomorrah.

Now let us take good note of this point, for it is of the greatest importance, and within it lies the crux of the matter. If God grant that I write this in such ink that everyone clearly imprint it in his heart, our dispute would be resolved forthwith. Let us note, I say, that however much a man refuses to acknowledge Christ and does not want to be a Christian (as in fact all those do not want to be who are not prepared to renounce themselves and crucify their flesh with all its desires), he can nevertheless not be put to death for that by the magistrate. If a miser, a braggart, a glutton or a drunkard who, in fact, by his whole life and deeds renounces Christ, nevertheless cannot (if he has not committed a civil crime) be put to death by the magistrate, I say that a heretic cannot either, for at worst he has but renounced Christ, effectually and by his deeds. If I am answered that a miser, a drunkard or a braggart at least acknowledges Christ by mouth, I may as well retort that a heretic does the same, but that both are but worse for it, for he is dishonest and hypocritical in doing so. And seeing that he in fact renounces Christ, it would be better if he were to do so by mouth as well, for then at least he would not be hypocritical, nor would he then by his hypocrisy lead anyone else astray. For which reason I say in conclusion that a heretic should no more be put to death than a miser, a drunkard or a braggart.

About Disadvantages

I am now going to talk about the disadvantages which could, it seems, come about if one should let the heretics live. These disadvantages could be twofold. The first, unrest and sedition, and the second, the false doctrine which the heretics might spread. To which I answer, firstly as far as the sedition is concerned, that the fools are bringing about that very evil which they think they are avoiding. For seditions are being caused by the fact that one wants to force and kill the heretics, rather than to let them live without constraint, for tyranny engenders sedition. It is for the moment certainly not necessary to quote old and remote examples to prove that this is so, for you are today carrying a more than adequate example of it in your bosom, O France. For it is certain that the sedition which torments you is the result of the tyrannising and persecuting of those which are held for heretics. Had they not been tyrannised, they would perhaps not have revolted. Or, at worst, if they had revolted, it would have gone no worse with you than it already has, and the princes would then have had a more justifiable reason for countering force with force, not because of the religion, but because of the sedition. God, who grants victory to whom He pleases, would then have favoured them more than He does, there where they are now in danger of falling into disgrace with Him. I do not even wish to mention that it would be better to be in danger of a future sedition than to use tyranny now, all the more so as tyranny is a far greater, certain and actual evil, which kills both the soul of the tyrant and the bodies and sometimes also the souls of the tyrannised, whilst sedition is an evil which may possibly not come about and which, if it does, can be repulsed or, at worst, will but affect the body.

As far as the false doctrine, which the heretics might sow, is concerned, I indeed admit that this is a disadvantage which it would be well to remedy. But one must take care (as I have just remarked, concerning the matter of sedition) that the remedy is not worse and more harmful to the patient than the ill which one desires to cure. Now it is a fact that the remedy which is being used, namely the tyrannising and murdering of the heretics, is far worse and more harmful than the illness. For in the first instance one but vexes and provokes them, so much so, that they are even more zealous to teach their heresy than they would otherwise have been. What is more, when the world so continually sees them cast in the role of martyrs, it comes to believe that they are good people, so that several will take up their cause, as the result of which you will sometimes for one make seven others. That, then, is the result of your foolish wisdom.

It also happens more often than not that, instead of persecuting a heretic, one by mistake persecutes a Christian. Christ indeed predicted this, when He said to His disciples that whoever would kill Him, would think that he was rendering service to God. This we always find to have happened, from the time of Christ, right up to our time. For firstly Christ and His Apostles and disciples were persecuted and murdered as heretics and later the martyrs were treated in the same manner. Since then, whenever there have been some unassuming and true Christians, they have always been persecuted as heretics. In our time, we who have adorned and embellished the tombs of the martyrs killed by our fathers, might, I very much fear, already have followed our fathers and made new martyrs, who will be honoured by our children. For more often than not truth is publicly ignored rather than accepted, and we are neither more fortunate nor more clairvoyant in this respect than our ancestors were. So much so, that if they failed in this respect (which we are forced to confess they did), we should guard ourselves from falling into their madness and blindness. Now this is such a great evil, that he who does not fear falling into it, indeed shows that he is a great fool, since he thus disdains the sound admonition of Christ. Of such fools speaks the wise Solomon when he says: "A wise man feareth, and departeth from evil: but the fool rageth, and is confident."[48] A wise man always chooses the lesser of two evils, if he cannot avoid them both. A wise doctor prefers to let the sickness continue, rather than to kill the patient. A wise labourer prefers to let the weeds grow with the corn rather than, whilst tearing out the weeds, to tear out the corn at the same time.

Jesus Christ, who is the wise doctor and labourer, saw this clearly in the parable of the tare, that is to say the weeds. For whether or not He speaks of heretics in this parable (I say this because this point is being debated), the circumstance is still similar. And even if Christ definitely did not speak of them, one who would speak of it in this manner, would but be speaking the truth. Likewise, if a labourer gave an order to his servants to the effect that they should tear the weeds out from amongst the corn, he would be acting foolishly (however much the weeds might be a nuisance, and however much it might be desirable for them to be torn out) and would cause the good corn to be pulled out. Thus a theologian who draws up an ordinance to the effect that one should kill heretics, is acting foolishly (however much the heretics may be a nuisance, and however much it may be desirable for them to be eradicated) and is causing Christians to be put to death. The experience (as has been shown hereabove) is more than enough proof of this. I take as witnesses in this matter those very ones who wrote books urging the killing of heretics who, holding themselves out to be Christians, confess that they are being persecuted and killed just like heretics; which would not happen if, in accordance with the above parable, one feared to tear out the corn with the weeds.

---

[48] Prov. 14:16.

In short, as the matter is such that Christianity encompasses so many sects today that one must be quite knowledgeable in order to be able to number them, each of which sects regards itself as Christian and the others as heretics, we are accepting a war such as the Midianites had,[49] if we accept the law regarding the persecution of heretics. We shall then but gnaw and eat each other until such time as, as Saint Paul says, we consume each other, which is an incomparably greater disadvantage than the other one. Regarding this point, someone will say to me: "Do you then want the heretics to be left to do and say whatever they please, without resisting them in any way?" Most certainly not, I do not want this, but it is my desire that they should be resisted by good and becoming means, like the wise and godly resisted them in the past. For I ask you how Jesus Christ resisted the Pharisees and Sadducees? How did the Apostles resist Simon, the magician, and Bar-Jesus and others? Was it not by means of divine and virtuous words, without putting the hand to the sword and without inciting anyone else, whether a public or private person, to do so? For they were wise warriors, who knew how to wage spiritual war with spiritual arms. They, therefore, who act differently and use violence, clearly show that they are not their followers.

The Ways to Resist the Heretics

Thus the way to combat the heretics would be by means of words of truth, which are always more powerful than words of lies. And if, having been persuaded by truth, and having been several times legitimately admonished, they still persevere with their hardheadedness, let them be excommunicated. That is the correct punishment for heretics. And if, having been excommu-

---

[49] Whom Gideon had fought (Judges 6 and 7). The Midianites, surprised by night, killed each other in the mêlée.

nicated, they still do not desist from teaching, let the people be forbidden to listen to them, and if someone nevertheless listens to them, let he himself be admonished and, in the end, should he persevere, be regarded as disobedient. That is how one can protect the church from heretics.

We see that this is the truth, for, apart from the fact that the Apostles of old thus protected their church, even today in Germany those who are called Anabaptists (who are, it seems to me, very gravely in the wrong), nevertheless uphold their church by these means, without any help whatsoever from the magistrate or the sword, so much so that even the most learned theologians cannot turn their people away from them. If they, being in error, nevertheless uphold their church through mere words against all the scholars, how much more could the true scholars, armed with the all-powerful words of Christ, who has promised them speech and wisdom against which none will be able to resist, not uphold the true Church against false doctrine? If after that the heretics should come to use force and to ferment sedition, then the princes and the magistrates will do their duty in giving armed protection to their subjects from whom they, for this reason, receive tribute-monies and salt taxes. The Turc indeed protects his Christian and Jewish subjects against the violence which could be done to them, and he does not protect them because of their religion, which he holds in disdain, but because they are his subjects. The Christian princes act likewise with the Jews. In this way they will be able to protect their subjects, whoever they may be, against any violence which might be done to them.

These are the correct ways to resist the heretics: by words, if they but use words, and by the sword, if they avail themselves of the sword. If it should accidentally happen (as it quite often does) that one who is not a heretic is excommunicated as a heretic, this disadvantage would be much less damaging than if, by the same error, he were to be put to death. For an unjust excommunication but harms the body, indeed sometimes it does not harm it at all, and it can easily be revoked. But death is an irrevocable ill.

Summary

Thus, to come to the point and to end my argument, I have shown that the cause of your illness, O France, is the forcing of consciences and that the remedies which are being sought for it, as much by the one side as by the other, are wrong and can but worsen and not cure your illness. Also they are displeasing to God, being against God and reason, not being based on a commandment by God, and without an authentic example, and proceeding only from a good intention, combined with ignorance of the truth. I have furthermore shown that the scruples which princes, who are urged by their mentors, feel about allowing the heretics to live, are not in accordance with God's wishes, and that these princes can, with a clear conscience and without sinning, allow the heretics to live and that this, moreover, involves incomparably less disadvantages and harm than to act otherwise.

Conclusion and Advice

Consequently, all things well considered and examined, the advice which I am giving you, O France, is the same which was given to you before by the booklet which I have referred to hereabove. If you had followed it, you would have avoided the miserable death of many thousands of your children, wisely predicted to you by the said booklet. That advice is that you should cease the forcing of consciences and stop persecution, not to mention the killing of a man because of his faith, and rather allow those who believe in Christ and who accept the Old and the New Testament, to serve God in your country, not in accordance with the beliefs of others, but in accordance with their own. If you act in this manner, there is hope that the God of mercy will have pity on you, and you will then find that, just as much as wrong advice and wrong remedies have hitherto been damaging to you, true advice and the true remedy will henceforth be of benefit to you.

Warning to the Preachers

As good advice is of no value to people if the governors are not in agreement with it, and as the governors cannot agree with it as long as they are being wrongly taught by those whose doctrine they follow, I advise you, O preachers and teachers, as much of the one side as of the other, to give this matter mature consideration and to remember the words of the Heavenly Teacher, who spoke as follows: "Blessed are the peacemakers, for they shall be called the children of God."[50] From this it clearly follows that the firebrands, who favour and incite war, are wretched, for they shall be called children of the devil. Do not think that it is a small scandal and sin to incite princes and nations to war. Think of the saying of the prophet Jeremiah, who calls the prophets murderers for having misled the people, and speaks to them as follows: "The kings of the earth, and all the inhabitants of the world, would not have believed that the adversary and the enemy should have entered into the gates of Jerusalem. For the sins of her prophets, and the iniquities of her priests, that have shed the blood of the just in the midst of her, they have wandered as blind men in the streets, they have polluted themselves with blood, so that men could not touch their garments. They cried unto them, Depart ye; it is unclean; depart, depart, touch not: when they fled away and wandered, they said

---

[50] St. Matthew 5:9.

among the heathen, They shall no more sojourn there."[51] These are the words of Jeremiah, by which he clearly calls the prophets and priests who had killed the innocents, not with their own hands, but had indirectly, through their false doctrine, been the cause of their death, blind men, murderers of innocent people and soaked in blood. For they had taught the people that they need not fear the Babylonians, and that God would preserve them from their tyranny and subjection. The people, consequently, trusting in this, rebelled against the Babylonians, and the king of Babylon, having been offended by this rebellion, beset and conquered them and treated the people in a deplorable way and murdered them. Of this killing, I say, Jeremiah accuses the prophets and priests, since they had, through their false doctrine, been the cause of it. Now consider how much more the preachers and teachers who expressly incite the people to arms in France today, can rightfully be called murderers, not to mention those who themselves take up arms and are to be found among the very first in the clash. I do not speak of all, for all are not like this. I speak of people like Ananias,[52] who will have to render account of their acts and whose number, please God, should not be greater than that of people like Jeremiah, and who should also have no more influence among the people and the princes.

To the Princes

Likewise, O Princes and Captains, be wise and rather follow the doctrine of the pacifists than that of the others, lest you, being blind, should follow the blind and fall with your guides into the abyss of perdition, from which those who have made you stumble into it, cannot retrieve you.

---

[51] Lament. 4:12–15.

[52] Ananias, who lied to God (Acts 5:1–10).

To the Private People

And you, private people, who are neither teachers nor lords, do not be so hasty to follow those who urge you to take up arms in order to kill your brothers, gaining nothing but the displeasure of God. For, certainly, those who are guiding you are leading you astray in this matter and are causing you to take steps for which they will veritably have to give account on your behalf. But even so, you will still not be acquitted, for both he who gives wrong advice and he who follows it, will be punished. May the Lord grant all of you the mercy to return, rather late than never, to your right senses, and if this should come about, I shall praise Him for it. If it does not come about, I shall at least have done ray duty, and I hope that at least someone will learn something, and realise that I have spoken the truth, which would mean, even if there be only one such person, that my work has not been in vain.

Written in the month of October, in the year 1562.